COURAGEOUS LEARNING

Finding a New Path through Higher Education

John Ebersole

and

William Patrick

HUDSON
WHITMAN
EXCELSIOR COLLEGE PRESS

Published by Hudson Whitman Publishing
Excelsior College Press
7 Columbia Circle, Albany, NY 12203-5159
www.hudsonwhitman.com
www.excelsior.edu

Library of Congress Cataloging-in-Publication Data
Ebersole, John, and Patrick, William.
Courageous learning: finding a new path through higher education /
John Ebersole and William Patrick. Includes bibliographical references.
ISBN: 978-0-9768813-1-5
Library of Congress Control Number: 2011930465
1. Education
2. Adult learners
3. Adult-serving postsecondary institutions

FIRST EDITION

Printed in China

Contents

"I think people want to have economic choices based on academic achievement, and we should be thinking about those. What you don't want to do is strip out the core skills of critical learning, creative learning, social learning, and what I would call courageous learning— which is the ability to learn how to learn, to have the guts to learn something new. I think those are the new four pillars of learning within the larger disciplines."

— Mark Milliron, The Bill & Melinda Gates Foundation

Introduction

Our nation is facing a great education crisis, and if we fail to respond quickly and seriously, we can expect our economy to grow weaker and our standard of living to decline. *Courageous Learning* is for those adults who, seeking to face this challenge, are considering returning to school, either to finish an undergraduate degree or to start a graduate one.

Knowing that a decision to return to school can be expensive and difficult, especially for those who may have been out of the classroom for decades, we have attempted to provide answers for some of the most common questions heard from returning students. We also profile five accredited institutions that offer excellent service and value to adult learners, and we outline ways for prospective students to find the right institution in terms of fit and cost. Each of these schools is non-profit, long-established, and focused specifically on the needs of adults.

In addition, we present the stories of several adult learners who have shown uncommon persistence in pursuit of their degrees. These stories were edited from interviews conducted within the last year. In their own words, these courageous learners describe the disparate challenges they have overcome, either to achieve personal and professional success or to transform themselves into productive members of society.

As you follow our assessment of the adult education landscape today, you will encounter varying numbers for those without a postsecondary degree or a high school diploma. The higher education leaders we interviewed, and the statistical sources we researched, gave us numbers that do not always align. For instance, depending upon the upper and lower ages of those included, the number of working adults with some college experience but no degree can vary by several million. However, there is little disagreement on the basic problem: we have tens of millions of working adults without a high school diploma or a college degree, and America has fallen considerably in the Organization for Economic Cooperation and Development (OECD) rankings when compared with other developed countries.

Your authors are William Patrick, a nationally recognized writer and instructor of writing, and John Ebersole, president of Excelsior College and a long-time administrator of adult education programs. Together, we have prepared a work that we hope will guide and inspire you.

If *Courage* is the quality of mind or spirit that enables one to face difficulty, danger, and pain with firmness and without fear, and *Learning* is knowledge or skill acquired by instruction, study, or experience, then *Courageous Learning* is the demonstration of mental or moral strength to venture into the world of lifelong learning, while withstanding fears of failure and the difficulties of life, in search of new skills and knowledge. Let us begin this journey with the story of a remarkable woman who embodies this spirit of courageous learning. In taking control of her own life, Marie Wrinn has made a profound difference in the lives of so many others.

– 1 –

Marie Wrinn:
No Child Dies Alone

Marie Wrinn was awarded Excelsior College's 2010 Robert E. Kinsinger Award, presented to a student with outstanding academic achievement who is involved with the non-profit sector. Marie recounts the surprising path that led her to found No Child Dies Alone, a non-profit service for caregivers of hospice patients.

I've been running my non-profit, No Child Dies Alone, pretty much by myself. I pay all my own expenses. I don't get paid for managing NCDA. Whatever funding we have goes for paying program costs. So to be recognized for that is like, "Wow, I guess I really am making a difference." The last time I got an award, when I was in elementary school, I passed out on the stage in front of everyone. I fell over. I won an award for perfect attendance at school, and I literally fell over. Afterwards, I said, "I'm never getting up in front of people again, even to talk."

But now I look back on the last few years and there's no way I could have planned the way it happened. The opportunities appeared, and there was just enough money to get by for each event. It wasn't like we had a million dollar endowment or some corporation said,

"Here you go. You can plan whatever you want." I had to make it happen, alone. As with my education, I had to decide that I was going to do it. I couldn't simply think about it and wish for it. I had to make it happen. But somehow, I've traveled to many countries and I have actually helped people.

I learned about moving around from my father. My dad was in the military, which meant we moved every one or two years. That was tough on a kid, trying to make friends and then leaving midway through every school year. And I learned about compassion from my mother. She started as a housekeeper, but that turned more into caregiving. She had elderly clients, and as they got sick and moved into nursing homes, she continued to see them. I played the violin, and when I was 12, I used to go with my mom and play "Twinkle, Twinkle Little Star" for the old people in their wheelchairs.

I got decent grades: As and Bs throughout high school. I qualified for the gifted-and-talented education program, but my parents were never around to take me to the extra classes off campus, so by the time I reached my senior year in high school, I didn't feel challenged and I was pretty bored with school. I was hoping for something better in college.

In 1992 I applied to the University of Arizona and was accepted, but I took only a semester and didn't continue. I wanted to be a veterinarian originally, but once I looked at the cost—at the time, about $15,000 a year—I knew I wasn't going to make it. I was living on my own, working restaurant jobs, flipping burgers and waitressing, job-hopping here and there. I couldn't qualify for loans because of the way federal financial aid was structured. As a working person, I made too much for the need-based scholarships, and I wasn't quite good enough for the merit scholarships. Getting married at 20 didn't help with my veterinary school dream either, because I had new obligations and less time. But I wanted to make better money than I was making.

Minimum wage wasn't much then, maybe three dollars an hour. So I started thinking about different career choices. Through my church, I was volunteering at a nursing home, doing a lot of stuff with the elderly. I started looking at the nursing program. I didn't know any nurses, I didn't know much about hospitals, and I didn't have any idea what nursing was about. I did know, from reading the ads though, that nurses got paid pretty well. So I took a nurse's aide certification course. At the time, it was like a mini-degree, a technical certification.

After that, I got a job as a nurse's aide, making about eight dollars an hour. That was cool. My very first job as a nurse's aide, after I finished that first six-month program, was at a home health/hospice. At the time, home healthcare and hospice were linked together as a healthcare benefit. My very first patient as a home health aide was someone with cancer. She was on hospice, and I didn't really know what that meant when I started. But I certainly saw how bad cancer was.

I spent two hours with her every day, bathing her and doing other things. She taught me a lot about dying. She was telling me about things she saw, about people, and about angels. She believed in a lot of complementary therapy, so I was there when her massage therapist came in, and also with the different family members. I was with her when she had pain. She usually slept a lot, and I was sitting there for two hours every day, so I would pull out the pamphlets about morphine and read them. That was my first real chance to see what caregivers go through with dying patients.

During that time, while I was working as a nurse's aide, I was observing what the other nurses were doing, and I thought, *Well, I still want to be a nurse.* Luckily, in Tucson, we had Pima Community College. I enrolled there in 1993, with plans to transfer to a university. However, they didn't accept me into their Associate's Degree of Nursing (ADN) program, the two-year RN program, at least not then. I was really good at my nurse's aide job and it was wonderful, so I kept working at that while I took general education courses and nursing prerequisites at Pima. But I also felt limited in my job, because I wanted to have more of an impact.

A year later, I reapplied to Pima's ADN program, but I still didn't get in. There were too many applicants for the number of slots available. I kept on taking prerequisite courses. They did have a Licensed Practical Nurse (LPN) bridge program. You took a certain number of courses and then completed an exam to be an LPN. Some of the credits for this program could count toward your ADN requirements. So I became an LPN and did that for a couple of years, working at nursing homes and in home health. However, I still wanted to do more.

It took six years before I was finally accepted into Pima's nursing program. By the time they let me in, it was 1998. It had taken so long that my credits kept expiring and I had to keep re-taking courses. Just to have something to show for all my work, I chose the Associate's Degree in General Studies. By the time I finished, I had amassed 128 credits for a degree that required only 60 credits.

Pima Community College had satellite campuses all over, so for the next couple of years, I traveled between various campuses to take all my nursing courses: anatomy and physiology, the nursing components, the theory, the assessments, the critical thinking, the hands-on nursing clinical rotations, and all the rest.

My husband had gotten a job in California, and I told him, "Yes, go west. It's a great opportunity. Try something different. Get out of your hometown." But I had one year left in my program, and if I had to transfer credits to California, it was clear I would have had to start all over. No way was I going to do that. I stayed in Arizona for a year, working full-time, finishing the last sets of courses, doing my clinicals, and preparing for my National Council Licensure Exam, the NCLEX.

I graduated on December 14, 2000, and I moved out to California the very next day. When I finished, I thought, *Now I can move, live with my husband, and start working as a registered nurse.* Once I had my associate's degree and my RN license, I figured I was done with school. I didn't need any further degree; I was making good money as a registered nurse. However, after working for a few years,

I started to apply for management jobs. What I wanted was the ability to work on a larger scale and to influence policy. It was that same kind of drive that said, "I want to affect change." I couldn't do that as a bedside nurse.

I started to see how things could be improved, but I didn't have that necessary credential that allowed people in charge to say, "Yeah, we trust your judgment on this." I had some supervising experience, but I wanted to be more than just a front-line manager. When they turned me down for jobs, saying, "Well, if you just had that degree, we would hire you," I realized it was the way of the world. Because I didn't have "the degree," I got less pay and was relegated to lesser duties. They didn't see me as having management potential.

I couldn't enroll in a California university, because they were too expensive. I was looking at the University of California at San Diego and at San Diego State, but the price had gone up to almost $30,000 a year. I expected to be able to transfer my credits, but neither school would accept much of my community college work. It was daunting. Then a friend asked me, "Have you heard of Regents College?" I had not, so I looked it up. It had become Excelsior by that time. I started to compare what it had to offer versus everyone else. What I really liked was, when I submitted my application, they accepted almost all my credits. I only needed something like 30 credits to complete my degree. That was cool. And I was looking at the credit per unit cost, and I said, "Okay, I think I can do this." It was still going to be like $15,000 to finish my degree, but that was compared to 30, 40, or even 50 thousand at a traditional school.

I applied and was accepted, but I realized it would still take me a long time to finish. I couldn't afford to take more than one class at a time. I was still working, and apart from that, I had gotten divorced. Things turned upside down, and I thought, *Wow, I really need to finish my degree now.* When I called the college, the encouragement I got was incredible. "Just keep trying," they told me. "Take whatever courses you can."

Excelsior gives you seven years to finish. Originally, I had enrolled in the RN to master's program, and even with their generous time allowance, some of my credits were going to expire. I decided to focus on completing my bachelor's degree. For that, some of the courses I needed, like "Teaching Across Cultures," were independent studies and weren't online. You had to find your own mentors and create your own experience. I thought, *I can't do that now. I don't know anyone. I just changed jobs. Who's going to mentor me? I can't do that kind of course.*

I lost all of my confidence for a while. I pushed a lot of things off and took a lot of exams and tested out of courses. I got the study guides and took the exams. *Pass the exams!* Passing was all I cared about then. A, B, or C: I didn't care what my grade was. I just needed to pass.

About then, I had grown tired of critical care nursing. I would do my rotation at the hospital and think, *Unh-unh, I don't like this craziness anymore.* At that time, the staffing levels were 1-to-15 for a 12-hour shift: one nurse to 15 patients. Not for me. In nursing homes, too, it was the same thing, but maybe with 40 or 50 patients. I had nurses who didn't show up for their shifts, so if you were the only nurse on the floor, you were responsible for the whole place until they found a replacement. I didn't get into nursing to do a bad job. I got into nursing because I cared about people, and I wanted to make a difference for people. Sitting there and worrying about whether you got every pill given on time wasn't the caring part of nursing.

I had recently moved again, to San Diego, and I was looking at another hospital nursing job, when an opportunity to work in hospice appeared. I really liked the idea of being able to focus one-on-one with patients again, and the job was for case management, so you had a group of people that you managed. I thought, *Cool. This is the kind of thing I want. You get to be in charge of something and you get to make a difference.*

When I started, the hospice work absolutely grabbed me. I loved it. One of the first patients I had as a case manager was a young woman with Lou Gehrig's disease, 40-some years old, on tube feeding, but she didn't want a ventilator. Of course, to be on hospice, that means you're terminal. This woman was declining fast, but she still had the tube feeding. She was having more and more trouble breathing. That's how Lou Gehrig's disease works: it progresses up from your feet until you can't breathe anymore, and then the next step is you need a ventilator. She didn't want that, and she could hardly talk anymore. She had two teenage sons and a husband. She had been the pillar of strength for all of them, and she had raised a lot of money for the ALS Foundation as well.

I've always felt that the best part of hospice nursing is the listening part—the ability to sit down and hold someone's hand and look into their eyes and say, "I can't fix this, but I'm here. I'll listen. What can I do? How can I support you right now?"

After a while, this woman told me, "I don't want the tube feeding anymore." She told this to me and to no one else, because she thought it was suicide to want that. Part of my understanding of nursing is that choosing to stop a treatment isn't about wanting to die: it's a signal to investigate the situation further.

Well, we worked through that. We asked a priest to come in, we got the doctor and the family to meet for a conference, and we decided to slow down the feeding and allow her life to progress more naturally into death. When she died, she was able to be with her family, in her king-sized bed, with her two sons and her husband right alongside her. We were able to allow her to die with dignity, and that's what I mean when I talk about effecting change and truly making a difference in someone's life, or death.

Until I was invited to her funeral after she died, I didn't realize how really important that difference was. What the family said about how I contributed to the process of helping her die made me understand. *Wow*, I thought, *this really is important work*. Heartwrenching, gut-wrenching, tears and everything—it was hard to receive recognition for doing something that I loved doing, especially when someone was dying. However, I really experienced what hospice caregivers had to go through, and I went on to get my hospice certification.

The hospice I was working at had some international outreach programs, and in May, 2007, some representatives from a hospice in Africa came to talk to us. A woman named Joan told us about the children's program they sponsored there and explained how, without morphine, they tried to help hundreds of kids who were dying with AIDS. Joan said these kids literally die in the streets, alone, if they're orphans, or if they've been kicked out of their homes. It was so horrible, and it made me wonder who was helping the caregivers there.

I had never really thought much about healthcare outside of the US, even though I had been on mission trips to other countries. But when Joan showed us this little building that houses these children while they're sick, receiving treatment, and dying, something clicked inside of me.

I started doing research about that program and I realized how much those people who worked with the dying kids needed help. I thought, *I'm going to raise some money for this hospice program.* And I started planning a community garage sale. At the same time, I was taking courses on self-empowerment, and doing a community project was part of it. Doing a garage sale and raising money for that hospice organization became my community project.

When I told my mom that I wanted to go to Africa, she started laughing and crying. I said, "What's wrong, Mom?" And she said, "When you were five years old, you came up to me and told me you wanted to be a missionary in Africa." I hadn't remembered that, but it was amazing how my life had come full circle.

Now things started to get going. I started dreaming bigger and planning bigger. If I was going to Africa, that community garage sale was never going to be enough. There was no way I could really look forward to making a difference in Africa with a single garage sale. I wasn't sure how to put it all together, but I decided I was going to start a non-profit. I didn't know anything about non-profit business, but I wanted to be in charge of something. I wanted to influence change. I wanted to affect policy development. I thought of a name and got it incorporated: No Child Dies Alone. That was actually the name of the community garage sale I started with, and it was how I advertised it.

During the process of setting up my non-profit, I ran into a wall of opposition:

"Well, that sounds like a good idea, but who are you?"

"So what if you're impassioned. You know how many millions of people would like to do this? You know how many people go and march for this or run for that? What makes you different?"

Not a lot of respect. Over and over, I heard: "You don't have the credentials."

I realized I had to finish my degree. I looked at the courses and at the requirements and thought, *I can do this!* All my life I had looked at school as something separate, not integrated with my life, where you really couldn't incorporate what you learned, or you couldn't find the time to drive to a campus. The last course I had taken on campus had been statistics, and driving there at six in the morning, trying to find parking, all to be there for only 45 minutes, was crazy. Excelsior's model worked a lot better.

I got my 501c3, non-profit corporate status approved on the first try, with no lawyer, but I still had to find a mentor and do another community project to finish my degree. So I just tied it all in. Teaching Across Cultures was one of my last courses. It was a practicum class, where you had to do a lesson plan and then get up and teach. My plan was to do a presentation at a conference in South Africa. I didn't want to start a hospice in another country, because I didn't want to do the same thing that other people were doing. I wanted to find that little area where I could contribute something, and I remembered the caregivers.

I worked on my presentation all through the course and then traveled to Africa. In September 2009, in Cape Town, South Africa,

I delivered my presentation: "Caregiver Wellness: We All Need It." It was meant to be all-inclusive—whether for a professional, like a working doctor, or for a mother taking care of her own child or nieces or nephews. They have to take care of themselves, too.

At the hospice Joan had described, I saw the foster parents and the staff workers, and the grueling job those caregivers have: they watch probably ten children die every month, and they have nothing more than Tylenol for the pain. I was glad I could offer them some alternatives, like massage therapy, that would help them and that they could use to help their patients.

My presentation went perfectly. All the preparation I had done for my class really paid off. They had told me, "Oh, maybe 30 will attend your class," but I was optimistic and had prepared for 50. In the end, 55 people showed up. I was an unknown, and I had no credentials, but I had a great idea. All the feedback said, "You're onto something here." After my presentation, people with 20 or 30 years of experience and advanced degrees were coming up to me and saying, "Wow, that's something I didn't know about. That's something new to me."

After I got my bachelor's degree, everything started to come together. The BSN degree would back up what I already knew. I had been so afraid in the beginning, when I was deciding whether I should go back to school or not. I kept thinking, *I can't do that*, but then I did it, and my life completely changed. It's great to write BSN after my name: Marie Wrinn, RN, BSN, CHPN (Certified Hospice Palliative Nurse).

I'm going to Honduras next month, and I have an eight-hour, full-day retreat for caregivers that I've designed. It's been translated into Spanish, and we're going to have simultaneous broadcasting. The event is limited to 100, but 160 have already registered. Just like in Africa, my focus will be on the need for caregivers to take care of themselves.

Because of hospice and because I went back and got my degree, the way that I look at life has changed: that whole living-life-now, pursuing-your-dreams-now idea. I have been trying to leave regrets behind, to not hang on to the past. I tell myself: *If you see an opportunity, go for it. If you fail, that's okay. You're trying. You're doing something. You're not being stagnant. Challenge yourself to do new things. If you don't take a risk, what's the point of living?* Through hospice, and through success with learning, my life has completely changed.

Remember my stage fright, where I passed out on stage in elementary school? Well, now here I am, not afraid at all, with something to say that makes a difference for people. It's something that seems simple and basic to me, but to people who haven't heard it, it's a gift. It has taken me my whole life to understand it, but now I can offer it to people all over the world.

– 2 –

Education in America: Pathways to Possibility

"Our yearlong examination of the challenges facing higher education has brought us to the uneasy conclusion that the (education) sector's past attainments have led our nation to unwarranted complacency about its future."
—The Spellings Commission, 2006

Why are so many people in America concerned right now about education? Everywhere you turn, the ways that children and adults learn or fail to learn have become everyday news items:

- In his 2011 State of the Union address, President Barack Obama called for America to once again produce the world's largest share of college graduates by the year 2020, urging us to "out-innovate, out-educate, and out-build the rest of the world."
- Facebook founder Mark Zuckerberg has pledged $100 million to help Newark's ailing public school system.
- Congress has been taking a hard look at for-profit colleges after a report by the Government Accountability Office detailed deceptive practices or fraud at the 15 colleges they visited.

- A TV star and former professional boxer has been subbing for a year as a tenth-grade English teacher in a large, inner-city Philadelphia high school for an Arts & Entertainment reality show: "Teach: Tony Danza."
- California's state university system has instituted massive cutbacks and raised tuition 32%, at the same time that almost all other states, faced with shrinking revenues and difficult-to-balance budgets, are following suit.

But the most buzz of all has come in the form of a recent movie about five elementary school kids.

Waiting for Superman is a documentary about public education from Davis Guggenheim, the director who focused attention on global warming in his Oscar-winning *An Inconvenient Truth*, featuring former Vice President Al Gore. Guggenheim's new movie tells the story of five children who attend failing public schools from Los Angeles to Harlem, of families who must endure a lottery to determine which kids will be selected to attend charter schools that are working, of unions and administrators that often stand in the way of these students and their parents, and of committed teachers and principals who are determined to make public education work.

Since its release in September 2010, *Waiting for Superman* has provoked a firestorm of response, positive and negative, as it should. It's about time that how we learn in America, from kindergarten through higher education, becomes everybody's business.

The cover of *New York* magazine asked, "Can One Little Movie Save America's Schools?" Oprah Winfrey featured the director on her show. Thomas L. Friedman, in an op-ed column in *The New York Times*, claimed that *Waiting for Superman* offers us the opportunity to see America from the "bottom-up, not from the top (Washington) down," and that what we will understand "is that there is a movement stirring in this country around education." In her criticism of the film, Randi Weingarten, president of the American Federation of Teachers, pointed out, "There are 3 million teachers and

133,000 schools in this country, and many of them do amazing, heroic work. I would have liked that kind of balance, so you could see good public schools doing a great job." She isn't wrong. We all know many examples of public schools that offer a terrific education. Yet our students at all levels—elementary through undergraduate—measured against many developed as well as developing countries, continue to perform poorly.

Early in December 2010, the Organization for Economic Cooperation and Development (OECD) issued the most recent scores from its Program of International Student Assessment (PISA), which tests 15-year-old students in 65 countries, and they show that the United States has slipped even further behind. Our students placed 17th in reading, 23rd in science, and 32nd in math. Shanghai, China, scored first in all three categories, and countries like Finland, Korea, Canada, Singapore, Japan, and Australia are consistently among the top ten. US Secretary of Education Arne Duncan said, "We have to see this as a wake-up call. I know skeptics will want to argue with the results, but we consider them to be accurate and reliable, and we have to see them as a challenge to get better. We can quibble, or we can face the brutal truth that we're being out-educated."

Many more dispiriting statistics and information underscore the fact that our public K-12 education system simply isn't doing its job well enough, and our younger generation is falling behind. However, if a poignant and timely documentary like *Waiting for Superman* is able to focus broad attention on this problem, we may improve the process of getting our schools back on track, keep more teenagers from dropping out of high school, and prepare more young adults to earn postsecondary degrees.

Waiting for Superman is much more than a film about what is wrong with elementary education in America. It's really a film about hope and about five children who believe that hope and learning are two concepts that can still live together. Early in the film, Daisy says that when she grows up, "I have a lot of choices. I want to be a nurse.

I want to be a doctor, and I want to be a veterinarian, because I just love animals and I want to help somebody in need."

We share Daisy's intrinsic hope and desire to help people, but perhaps less innocently. We are aware that our K-12 educational system has terrible, entrenched problems that resonate through our culture and threaten our future. It isn't hard to see how those problems snowball through the secondary years and, more often than not, contribute to long-lasting occupational limitations for millions of American workers who may never learn to read properly, or who drop out early, or who fail to develop the skills necessary to succeed in our fast-paced world. The film tells us that a student drops out of high school every 26 seconds. What does the future hold for people without the skills and training needed to find decent jobs as they get older? Taken one by one, the stories of lower-achieving adults run the gamut from disappointing to tragic, but taken together, they weaken our economy and our spirit while threatening to keep America from resuming its place as a world leader in education.

What makes the new dialogue about education especially important is that it has the potential to move a long-running, jargon-filled debate about learning away from academic venues and into a more mainstream discussion not only in state legislatures but at kitchen tables across the country. Suddenly, a lot of people are vitally interested in what's happening with learning and with our children. As the film opines, we cannot continue to place the future of our children in the hands of luck.

Dennis Jones, president of the National Center for Higher Education Management Systems (NCHEMS), has measured the cycles of American education for over forty years, and he feels a huge shift is under way: "You can quarrel with Obama's goal, but I find it really refreshing that there is one—that somebody is paying attention—and that there is a conversation about the importance of higher education," Dennis said. "Going back even 15 years, I would go and sit in front of a legislative committee in someplace like

Arkansas and talk about the importance of higher education, and you could just see the *No Sale* signs going up. Now they're saying, 'Hey, we have to improve education here. It's absolutely a necessity. How are we going to do it? What should we be doing to improve access and success for students in higher education in Arkansas?' Now they get the importance of it."

It's hard to deny that our K-12 public education system is struggling on many levels, but we believe we have an even greater educational problem in this country that has been hiding in plain sight: many Americans no longer know enough to compete effectively for the jobs of the future. Our workforce, like our 15-year-old PISA test-takers, is falling behind the rest of the world, and our lack of education is one of the primary reasons for it. We *are* being out-educated and out-worked, and if we don't do something about it, and quickly, our standard of living will be drastically altered in the near future.

The Lumina Foundation, a private foundation based in Indianapolis, warns that the college-attainment gap will continue to widen as America's most-educated generation, those currently between 55 and 64, moves into retirement, and that we are likely to face an unprecedented shortage of college-educated workers by 2020. For the past 40 years, the proportion of our population with a two- or four-year college degree has remained at about 39%. More and more, though, other nations are reaching higher attainment rates, some as high as 54% in their population of 25- to 34-year-old workers. Today, the United States has dropped to 10th place in the percentage of its young adult population with college degrees.

Pat Callan, President of the National Center for Public Policy and Higher Education, sounds a similar alarm: "Our largest and best-educated group of Americans is the baby boomers. However, as we speak, they are moving toward retirement. So we're now in an international, highly-competitive, global economy, and who is going to take the places of these people? If we look at our 25–35-year old workforce, in the OECD international comparisons that don't even include China and India, we're one of only two countries in which the younger population is not better educated than the older population. The rest of the countries have made their gains more recently. We made ours in the 1950s, 60s, and 70s. They've made theirs in the last decade and a half. Their educational strength is in their young population, who will be in the workforce for the next 40 years."

These educational problems aren't new. In the fall of 2006, then-Secretary of Education Margaret Spellings and her Commission on the Future of Higher Education first shone a spotlight on the fact that America does not have the educated workforce it needs to compete in a global economy. Among their findings:

- Many other countries are educating more of their citizens to more advanced levels than we are.
- Many high school graduates do not enter college because of inadequate information and rising costs, combined with a confusing financial aid system that spends too little on those who need help the most.
- A troubling number of high school graduates who do make it to college waste time and taxpayer dollars to master English and math skills they should have learned in high school.
- A sizeable number never complete their college degrees, in part because some colleges and universities don't accept responsibility for making sure that those they admit actually succeed.
- There are disturbing signs that many who earn degrees have not actually mastered the reading, writing, and thinking skills we expect of college graduates.
- Between 1996 and 2006, literacy among college graduates has actually declined. Unacceptable numbers of college graduates enter the workforce without the skills employers say they need in an economy where knowledge matters more than ever.

These disturbing pronouncements were made before the current recession began, before the unemployment rate reached almost

10%, and before tuition and housing costs increased to astronomical levels at many traditional institutions of higher learning. Margaret Spellings recently addressed some of these issues with us:

"I created the Spellings Commission—now about five-plus years ago—to start to think about these things, when it was quite unfashionable and when nobody was talking about them. I can tell you that I've had a number of people say to me, 'Wow, I wish we had listened then.' We love to run around saying we're the finest in the world. And that is true. I think we have the finest higher education system in the world. But the question is not that. The question is: Is it fine enough for the changing world that we're entering into? We've always done a darn good job of educating elites. We sure have. But that is increasingly not the game."

The education game has changed: 18- to 22-year-olds who live on campus now comprise less than 20% of the college students in this country, and the cost of a private undergraduate education at some four-year colleges has risen to far more than the price of the average home sold in 2010. Sending a son or daughter to college is one of the most important and expensive decisions a family is going to make, and as Margaret Spellings points out, many times that decision is ill-informed.

"We often have more information about our cup of coffee than we do about this decision," she said. "Our kids 'get a feeling' about a certain school, and the next thing you know, you're hundreds of thousands of dollars in debt. We haven't provided families with much information about college. What we have provided is more around inputs, mood, and optics than substantive information. I think our consumers are starting to demand more. They want to know, rightly, what kind of outcomes they can expect for their investment."

The vast majority of our colleges and universities are committed to educating a diverse cross-section of students to improve the quality of their lives. These schools provide students with tools that can broaden their intellectual abilities, strengthen their participation as conscientious citizens, and help them prepare for their careers. Whether conveying essential information at a picturesque campus or through distance learning, most of the people who work in public and private American schools of higher education are dedicated to achieving excellence for themselves and others.

However, most traditional schools, hampered by the necessity to schedule class times and to maintain expensive physical campuses, have their hands full taking care of their normal populations of 18- to 22-year-olds. They have not been structured or oriented to serve the needs of working-age adults. Yes, many have evening degree programs, but those programs remain time-and-place specific. Some offer online courses, and that certainly helps. But these schools are often reluctant to assess prior learning or accept significant credit in transfer. Many adult learners do not have the physical proximity or flexible schedules to attend these traditional programs, nor the ability to afford the costs of a degree at some of these schools. Also, most institutions of higher education also have sound economic reasons, as well as academic quality issues, for not wanting too much work to be done somewhere else.

This creates a space in the marketplace for the institutions that we profile in Chapter 6. All five of these schools serve the new majority of American students — adult learners — and all five are doing pioneering work in providing new ways for adults to earn a degree. By validating prior learning, aggregating learning from both academic and non-academic sources, removing barriers to credit transfer, and focusing on learning outcomes rather than on time spent in class, these institutions are providing new models for degree completion.

The Other 80% of College Students

In Chapter 1 we met Marie Wrinn, the first of five Excelsior College graduates who, in their own words, describe how they overcame substantial obstacles to earn a degree and how they put their hard-earned education to work for them. Her story is unique in its specific aspects, but her persistence and instinct to help others are courageous tendencies shared by many of us. Throughout her career, Marie has searched for different and rewarding ways to express her intuitive call to service. The courses she took to earn a degree showed her the way to expand her vision and to follow a pragmatic, if post-traditional, means of achieving it.

However, if we were asked to imagine a typical college student, would Marie be someone we think of first? Probably not. She isn't a 20-year-old with a backpack, hurrying across a picturesque quad to her 10 a.m. sociology lecture, nor is she the star center on a Division I women's basketball team. Like most adult learners, Marie has had to juggle jobs and family responsibilities with the demands of pursuing her education.

Arthur Levine, former president of Teachers College, Columbia University, and current president of the Woodrow Wilson National Fellowship Foundation, articulates the educational reality we now face: "The 18- to 22-year-olds who are attending full-time and living on campus now constitute under 20% of all college students. So are they receiving a strong education? Yeah, those students are probably receiving the best education we have. The real challenge is the other 80%. Older students. The new majority—older, part-time, over 25. They say that what they want out of college is convenience (offer classes at a time when they're available); good service (the registrar is actually there to help them); and financial aid should be more predictable than playing the lottery. What they're saying is, 'I want quality instruction, and I want low cost.'"

So who is this new majority in our country? They are people over 22 who attend school to earn degrees, to acquire new knowledge and competencies, to become better citizens, to qualify for higher-skilled jobs, and to fulfill their educational dreams. The National Center for Education Statistics defines these post-traditional, adult learners as students who fall into one or more of the following categories:

- They attend school part-time.
- They are financially independent of their parents.
- They include those who have no high school diploma or have not passed General Educational Development tests (GEDs).
- They are employed full time.
- They have delayed enrolling in a postsecondary school past the first year after high school graduation.
- They have dependents other than a spouse.

Malcolm Knowles, one of the pioneers of adult education in the United States, characterized adult learners as autonomous and self-directed, with a foundation of life experiences and knowledge that may include previous education, family responsibilities, and work-related training and activities. He defined them as goal-oriented, relevancy-oriented, and practical: they know what they want to achieve from any given course, and they expect the learning in that course to relate pragmatically to their jobs and their lives. And finally, Knowles acknowledged the importance of according respect to adult learners for the wealth of experience they can add to the classroom.

The Rochester Institute of Technology, echoing some of Knowles's findings on their online learning website, contrasts adult learners with traditional, younger students based on the general learning characteristics of each group:

Adult Learners	Adolescent Learners
Problem-centered; seek educational solutions to where they are compared to where they want to be in life	Subject-oriented; seek to successfully complete each course, regardless of how the course relates to their own goals

Results-oriented; have specific results in mind for education — will drop out if education does not lead to those results because their participation is usually voluntary	Future-oriented; youth education is often a mandatory or an expected activity in a youth's life and designed for the youth's future
Self-directed; typically not dependent on others for direction	Often depend on adults for direction
Often skeptical about new information; prefer to try it out before accepting it	Likely to accept new information without trying it out or seriously questioning it
Seek education that relates or applies directly to their perceived needs, that is timely and appropriate for their current lives	Seek education that prepares them for an often unclear future; accept postponed application of what is being learned
Accept responsibility for their own learning if learning is perceived as timely and appropriate	Depend on others to design their learning; reluctant to accept responsibility for their own learning

Louis Soares, in his June 2009 report "Working Learners: Educating Our Entire Workforce for Success in the 21st Century," defines working learners as "individuals already in the workforce who currently lack a postsecondary credential and are needed wage earners for themselves and their families." He goes on to say that, "A working learner can be married or single, male or female, or a child living with a parent whose earnings are critical to family income. If these working Americans are to obtain a postsecondary credential, they will have to combine learning, employment, and family responsibilities with their working lives."

He includes 18- to 24-year-olds whose income is critical to helping support their families in his postsecondary pool of working learners who currently have no postsecondary credential and are not enrolled:

18- to 24-year-olds who are not high school graduates	3.2 million
18- to 24-year-olds with a high school diploma but no college	6.8 million
18- to 24-year-olds with a high school diploma and some college	2.8 million
25- to 64-year-olds who are not high school graduates	11.8 million
25- to 64-year-olds with a high school diploma but no college	36.2 million
25- to 64-year-olds with a high school diploma and some college	14.2 million

Total 75 million

*Working Learners, June 2009

However, in its 2007 Report, "Returning to Learning: Adults' Success in College is Key to America's Future," the Lumina Foundation posited that, in spite of the vast pool of working learners without postsecondary credentials and regardless of their importance to American life and well-being, "adult learners have typically been treated as an afterthought in higher education." Because they must struggle to balance work with family commitments, they are at greater risk of failing to complete their courses and degrees. Frequently, they cannot secure traditional financial aid, which most often is reserved for younger, full-time students. Millions of adult learners work for their degrees in a higher education system that has been designed for traditional students who build their schedules around time-and-place specific courses. And whether they enroll in community colleges or four-year institutions, adult learners are often forced to follow less-conventional pathways such as continuing-education or online programs at traditional institutions. Many seek more expensive degrees at profit-driven, corporate-owned institutions, which offer distance-learning programs more suited to working adults who are unable to attend time-and-place fixed classes.

In an October 2010 report, "Degree Completion beyond Institutional Borders: Responding to the New Reality of Mobile and Nontraditional Learners," Louis Soares, along with Rebecca Klein-Collins and Amy Sherman of the Council for Adult and Experiential Learning (CAEL), have pointed out that, "More than 60% of college students transfer at least once in their undergraduate programs, and an increasing number of students possess college-level knowledge and skills from their work and life experience. The thousands of military personnel needing to make the transition to civilian jobs after service in Iraq and Afghanistan may also have college-level skills and knowledge that they have acquired during their time in service."

The more we search, the more we find impediments to learning for adults who have returned to school. Many are enrolled in programs that are not documented by traditional postsecondary data-collection systems. Thus, it may be impossible to determine how effectively these challenges scare off prospective adult learners. But this group is the client pool we need to reach if we are to succeed in meeting President Obama's goal for degree completion.

CAEL, in partnership with the National Center for Higher Education Management Systems (NCHEMS), has published an eye-opening report, "Adult Learning in Focus," that reveals the following:

- In the United States, more than 59 million people, or 30% of the adult population, are untouched by postsecondary education—and in 35 states, more than 60% of the adult population does not have an associate's degree or higher.
- Over 26 million adults in the United States currently have no high school diploma, more than 32 million have not attended college and are earning less than a living wage, and over 8 million have not attended college and speak little or no English.
- 32 states cannot catch up to the educational attainment levels of the best-performing countries internationally by relying solely on strategies related to traditional-aged students.

While higher education experts may include different at-risk groups in their figures, the data clearly point to a vast pool of under-utilized talent and potential in our adult population. To meet the president's goal, we can't wait to tap into that pool. We urgently need to increase the number of adults with college degrees, because our under-25 population alone cannot sustain us economically during the next decade.

George Keller, in his recent book *Higher Education and the New Society*, reveals that fertility rates in developed countries have been steadily declining for the last twenty years: "Except for most countries in Africa and much of the Middle East and Southeast Asia, birth rates are now declining in nearly every country." Keller goes on to explain that this decline in the fertility rate is the most rapid in world history, and if present trends continue, global depopulation could begin by the year 2050. In the United Nations Population Division's 2002 biennial compendium, fertility rates in Italy, Britain, and the United States were 1.21, 1.7, and 2.05 respectively, while rates in countries like Somalia, Uganda, Yemen, and Pakistan ranged between 5 and 8.

What that means is our population in America is inexorably shifting. As our birth rate declines and our medical care improves, people will live longer. "By the year 2030," Keller tells us, "the population of Americans over 65 years of age is predicted to double from 35.5 million persons in 2000 to roughly 70 million, and in 2030, the country will be home to more persons over 65 than under 18."

Young people are less likely to go to college, or stay in college because they come from divorced or single-parent families, research shows. Additionally, more and more young people arrive at college unprepared to learn because they never absorbed the basics of reading, writing, and mathematics in their K-12 years, the majority of college professors now report. Thus, there are simply not enough young people completing college, earning degrees, and gaining the skills they will need to be competitive in the twenty-first century workforce. The conclusion becomes obvious: we need adult learners to fill the gap.

During the second half of the twentieth century, the American economy continued to generate millions of middle-class jobs that required no college-level knowledge or skills. Sons and daughters followed parents into manufacturing, construction, public safety, and small-business jobs, among many other occupations, that afforded them a standard of living that most of the world envied. Since the outsourcing and Internet development of the 1990s, however, that reality has largely changed. Global competition has ensured that many less-skilled manufacturing jobs, as well as many higher-skilled clerical ones, have moved to other countries. Lower-skill jobs continue to exist in America, of course, but the workers in those jobs are less able to buy a house, afford health insurance, send their children to college, or even to remain in the middle class. Access to middle-class jobs demands, more often than not, some kind of higher education.

In June 2010, Anthony Carnevale, a labor economist at Georgetown University's Center on Education and the Workforce, published a provocative report, "Help Wanted: Projections of Jobs and Education Requirements Through 2018." In that report, Carnevale explained that he set out to provide a detailed forecast of jobs and their education requirements because the job landscape will change significantly as the current recession weakens and new jobs replace the ones that were lost since 2007: "The emphasis of the recovery will be largely on skilled jobs," he informs us. "Many people who lost jobs that required only a high school education or less will find that their relatively low-skill jobs will not come back at all, lost to automation or overseas competitors. Scores of these job seekers will be left behind because the jobs that survived the recession and the jobs created in the recovery will require postsecondary education or training. The economy that emerges from the recession will be different than the economy that preceded it. The industrial economy

of the twentieth century has slowly transformed itself into a new services economy that demands more education and different skills of
its workers."

Undersecretary of Education Martha Kanter traveled with President Obama's entourage to Warren, Michigan, in the summer of
2010, at the height of the recent automotive manufacturing layoffs.
She met there with some of the workers who were losing their
assembly-line jobs at the Chrysler Stampings Plant and saw the sad
proof of what Carnevale's report is predicting.

"It was heartbreaking. They were closing the assembly line, but
there were going to be jobs in robotics. However, the literacy levels
and the training required to be successful in this modern economy
were just not there," she explained. "The education gap is so huge.
These are people 40 to 50 years old, and older, and they would have
to go back to school to get a new career. And when you consider that
of the 300 million Americans, plus or minus, we have 93 million who
have had little or no college, you know that some of them are going
to be able to do it, but the bulk of them are not. Shame on us for not
educating the last generation in the way that we should have. We
need to let people transfer their skills across economic opportunities, so you wouldn't get stuck in an assembly line job for 25 years
and then have nowhere to go in a downturn. I think we can do better than that."

In "Working Learners," Louis Soares makes a strong case for
going further than the changes President Obama proposed for Pell
grants and the unemployment insurance system, which would help
to make postsecondary education more accessible to greater numbers of adults: "These 'working learners' are now served by a system
that is overly focused on crisis intervention at the point of unemployment and getting people back into jobs, and not focused suffi-
ciently on the need for on-going training and education."

Soares goes on to define our current postsecondary system of
education as bifurcated: "On the one hand are the tightly-structured,
traditional college programs that serve the needs of full-time students

who are ushered through the system toward completion of a college degree. This system, however, is ill-suited to workers who receive their education over longer periods during their work and family lives, and during occasional gaps in employment. On the other hand, there is a more flexible workforce development system, but it provides an unstructured hodge-podge of training that often fails to lead to a well-conceived career path and that produces little in the way of meaningful academic credentials for either the worker or the employer."

Pat Callan of the National Center for Public Policy and Higher Education articulates our current education-to-workforce dilemma: "In the post-WWII era, when we educated more people to higher levels than we had ever done before, people who didn't get a college education could still, if they had a good work ethic, get a job in a factory making automobiles or steel and have a middle-class income and buy a house in the suburbs and send their kids to college. That's the part of America that has disappeared.

"When we decide now about who gets college opportunity, we're really deciding on who has a chance to be in the middle class, and that changes in a very fundamental way the relationship between higher education and American society. We never designed our educational system to play that role, but that's what, basically, the marketplace is telling us, and that's what the public gets, I think, better than the educational and political leadership."

Mark Milliron, Deputy Director for Postsecondary Improvement for The Bill & Melinda Gates Foundation, agrees that people are rightly concerned about our educational system, and he laments that "we are on the precipice of having the first generation which is less educated than the one that preceded it. The canary in the coal mine, I think, is there."

However, Milliron takes a longer, historical view of American education, and he believes we are currently witnessing the reorganization of our educational system around our economy and our society: "I am increasingly frustrated by people who assume that American education doesn't change. American education, in general, has done good work to try to adjust to our economic and societal realities. I think, in the last 40 years, we have been responding, on the societal side, to a real push for social justice, and on the economic side, the real push for more people to begin new economies. You saw the creation of new models of education for adult learners with schools like Regents/Excelsior and Empire State and others. I think a lot of that was in response to the idea that we should give anybody and everyone a pathway into higher education. That was made even more acute, I think, in the late '80s and early '90s, as we began to move pretty forcefully from an industrial economy into the Information Age.

"Now I think we're at a place where we realize that access is important, but it absolutely is not sufficient. I think we're realizing now that completion has to be a part of the equation. It's not good enough to get people to higher education—to postsecondary education. You've got to get them through. So certification, diplomas and degrees matter, because they give people choices, and because they give people pathways to possibility."

Pathways to possibility is a particularly astute term, as well as an emotional necessity, for adult learners. So often, with the responsibilities that attend work and personal life, it becomes especially difficult for working adults to envision a way out of challenging situations.

– 3 –

Daniel Tulip:
A Touch of Grace

*Daniel Tulip's story demonstrates how important encour-
agement can be for adult learners. In 2010, he won Excelsior's Robert P. Mahoney Award, given to a student who
completes a degree in the face of significant challenges,
while demonstrating a dedication to community and vol-
unteer service. Through three deployments to Iraq and
despite a serious illness, Dan persevered to earn his degree.
The understanding of his advisors and consistent support
of his wife, Marcie, were key elements in his success.*

I started taking classes when I first went into the military, back in
October 1988. That was before distance education had become popular. I took classes wherever I was stationed, and it was hard because
I was full-time, and active duty the whole time. I'll never forget—I
took my first college class and I got an A and I thought, *How did this
happen?* Maybe it was because I read the book and because I did all
my assignments, unlike in high school. I also knew I'd be held financially responsible if I didn't pass the class. The Army only reim-
burses you for the courses you pass.

I went to Fort Drum, New York, in October 2002, and within a
few months of arriving there, the Iraq buildup started. I was deployed
there in March 2003 for the first rotation. After I came back from

that first deployment, I knew I was getting to the point where I was going to retire in a few years, and I realized I needed to do something to get my bachelor's degree. At that time, I had over 100 credit hours, but they were from a college here, there, and everywhere. I went to the education center and met with Les Barbour. I'm sure he's still at the Fort Drum Education Center. He told me about Excelsior. He said, "Hey, look, why don't you have them do an audit on everything you've taken and see where you stand?"

I did that and, sure enough, I was within about 24 credits of getting a bachelor's degree. They told me they'd accept all the classes I had taken and all of my military training. So I started with them, but then I went back to Iraq two more times. It was hard, because I was often in some remote locations where we lived in close quarters. I didn't really have any privacy. I literally had to stay up late at night, when everyone else was asleep, so I could study. That was the only quiet time I had. During the day, there was just too much commotion and noise. I would wake up at 4:30 or 5 in the morning and read or write papers. Then I'd wait until the end of the day to send correspondence to my professors. We always had e-mail capability.

For that first deployment—March 2003 until February 29, 2004, leap day—I didn't come home. When I did rotate back to the States, I was again stationed at Fort Drum, above Syracuse, New York, 28 miles south of the Canadian border and 375 miles from my hometown of Greenwood, Pennsylvania. Whenever I could, I would drive home for weekends to see my three kids. That was a long trip for just a weekend, but they were young then—6, 8, and 13—and I tried to go see them whenever I could.

In October 2004, I was home for my birthday, and I was feeling sorry for myself because I was divorced, and because I knew I'd be going back to Iraq again. My sister made me go out anyway, and she introduced me to this really attractive woman named Marcie, who was also divorced. I said, "Do you need to get a drink?" and she said, "Yeah, it's my birthday. My girlfriend wants to buy me a drink." And then I said, "Well, it's my birthday, too." But she figured it was some pickup line and said, "Get out of here—your birthday's October 9th?" And I said, "No, it's October 10th." Then she said, "Well, today's the 9th," but when I looked at my watch, I saw that it was after midnight. So hers was officially over and mine had started.

"How old are you?" she asked me, and I told her, "36." Then she said, "Don't you want to know how old I am?" and I said, "No, not really."

"I think I better tell you—I'm 45," she said. I just couldn't believe that. I told her, "Forget it, you're not 45," and I asked to see her license. She couldn't believe I was ID'ing her, but hey, I was a military cop, and I swear she looked about 25.

The three of us—me, Marcie, and her girlfriend, Patty—sat and talked until 1:30. I told her I was in the Army, and I had gone to high school in Greenwood. Then she told me her dad was a teacher and football coach at the high school: Frank Amato. I couldn't believe it. "Oh, my God, I had your dad in high school," I responded. I was of course terrified of him. He was my football coach and also my social studies teacher. I was thinking, *How can I possibly go on a date with one of Frank Amato's daughters? Whoa!*

Growing up, I was never held accountable for anything I did. No supervision. When I was 12 years old, my brother and I had to work to pay for our parents' bills. I rode a bike to get to my jobs. We were really poor, but I refused to take free lunches when I was in school as a teenager. I got my driver's license on my own; I bought my own clothes. I would even buy clothes for my siblings. I didn't apply myself in school because no one expected me to. I did go out and wrestle one year and I did really well.

My high school GPA was 1-point-something. I can remember being halfway through my senior year, and I had to go to the office more than once. I had skipped so much school to go to work, or I'd just go and do whatever I wanted to do, and no one ever questioned me. There was no accountability. I went to the office one time and I said, "I need to get a copy of my schedule." This was in January. And they said, "Why do you need a copy of your schedule?" and I said,

"I'm not really sure where I'm supposed to be right now." They looked hard at me and said, "Okay, just have a seat right over there."

But finally I got a job working on a farm, and the guy who ran the farm—James Wood—he became a big inspiration for me. He changed everything for me. I mean, he was my role model. He could do everything. You've heard the expression "Jack of all trades, master of none"—well, this guy was a master of all trades. I'd get frustrated by something, and he'd walk up and he'd have it done in a second. He taught me that when you do something, you do it right the first time and you put 110% into it. He really pushed me. When I went into the Army, I went from working on a farm, making three or four dollars an hour in the late '80s, straight into military life, where I applied that same work ethic. I got rewards, and I got promotions, and I just took off. I went from a private E1 to a senior noncommissioned officer in nine years. I thrived in the Army.

But back to that night of my birthday. The three of us sat and talked, and I said, "I come home once or twice a month. Do you mind giving me your number? I'd like to take you out to dinner." And she got scared, but Patty told her, "Come on, Marcie, you can tell he's a nice guy. Give him your number," and she did. I called her later that week, and we were on the phone Thursday night and Friday night for about three hours, nonstop until midnight, and then I drove back down on Saturday.

I learned later on that Marcie was thinking, *I'm getting involved with a guy who's five and a half hours away, and he's probably going back to Iraq.*

A few weeks before I met Marcie, I had been in an accident. I used to race bicycles. I raced US Cycling Federation road races; I was ranked 12th in New York State. I mean, I would race at speeds upward of 35 or 40 miles per hour. I had gotten picked up by a sponsor, a local bike shop, and I was doing really well. I was climbing up the competitive ladder, and then I got hit by a car.

I was out on a training ride in Watertown, going about 25 miles an hour. I was trying to get a good long ride in before dark. I was in the bike path, and no one was in the turn lane, and then all of a sudden this car veered suddenly into me. I hit the car so that one foot was above the bumper and the other foot was below it, and I rolled across the hood and went into the windshield. Then I flew across the intersection — one of those huge, multiturn intersections.

I went to the hospital, and because I was in such good shape from cycling — I weighed about 170 pounds and had less than 10% body fat — it seemed like nothing was seriously wrong. I had no broken bones, nothing serious, just a lot of bruising and some scraped-up skin. But it sure hurt when I walked for a week to ten days after. The accident happened September 21st, and I met Marcie October 9th, right after my bruises healed.

A little over a month into our relationship, right before Thanksgiving, I called Marcie on the phone and told her I was peeing blood — fire-engine-red blood. I had gone to an urgent care clinic, and they detected a shadow on the ultrasound. Marcie was a nurse, so she knew all the ways that could mean trouble. She told me to go see a civilian urologist. They didn't have a military urologist at Fort Drum, so they let me choose one I wanted. I got referred to a professor of urology at Syracuse University. Before I even went to see him, he told me he wanted me to get a CAT scan. I did, and the CAT scan was clear. But my urologist wanted to do exploratory surgery anyway.

I was thinking, *The CAT scan was clear, and it was probably an error on the ultrasound, so they'll do some minor surgery to see if everything is okay and I'll be out quick.* I woke up from surgery to a nurse telling me, "The surgery went fine. They removed a tumor from your bladder." And I said, "Wait, time out." I mean, I freaked right there. I was very emotional.

Turned out there was a malignant tumor in my bladder, but it was "low-grade, non-invasive." But it was trying to attach to the wall, and it was going from what they call stage 0 to stage 1. The urologist told me the bleeding had more than likely resulted from internal bruising suffered in the bike accident, and he said if I had not been hit, I would never have known that I had bladder cancer.

He also told me, "There's only one or two ways you get this kind of cancer. Either you're a heavy cigarette smoker for 30 or 40 years, or you've been exposed to chemical or industrial agents." Well, hello—there's no doubt in my mind that I had been exposed to industrial and chemical agents. I'm not talking about chemical warfare. But during my first deployment, we were at one location in Iraq for a good period of time, and it smelled like radiator fluid every day. We later learned that the Iraqis don't have any pollution controls; they'll just dump toxins in the river. We found literally dozens of these enormous bunkers where they stored 55-gallon drums of industrial goop. This stuff was constantly emitting into the air. We were breathing it every day. It would not surprise me if, 10 to 15 years from now, a lot of soldiers start to come out of the woodwork with problems. So, if it weren't for the accident and the subsequent operation, I would have gone back to Iraq for my second deployment and would have probably come back home with stage 1 or stage 2 bladder cancer. Who knows what my chances would have been with that? But here's the ironic thing. At that intersection where I got hit in Watertown, there was a religious memorabilia shop called A Touch of Grace, and on the side of that building is an angel overlooking the intersection. I'm not kidding.

I had the surgery in December, and then I went back to Iraq the next October. Our unit received a deployment notice and, as far as the military was concerned, I was not being treated for anything. I had a surgery; the cancer was removed; I was fully deployable. But it was scary for me to go back to Iraq the second time. I was afraid to breathe. Was I going to get cancer again? On top of all that uncertainty, I was also afraid Marcie was going to leave me, too. That was a pretty stressful time.

The first time I was in Iraq, I had been awarded the Combat Action Ribbon. We were engaged by machine-gun fire. We were downtown in Mosul, and the locals learned that we had captured one of Hussein's sons. The whole city went a little crazy. There were a lot of demonstrations. They would toss rocks and everything else at us.

A few days later, it went really nuts and they were throwing bullets, not rocks, in every direction. I was part of a quick reaction force that had to go into Mosul to reinforce a police station. We had a squad inside surrounded by about 700 people. We had to work our way in with helicopters, but we finally got in and got them back to the base safely. However, it wasn't without us getting shot at quite a bit. They were lighting us up. In the city, you can't tell where the fire is coming from. You couldn't just open up on the whole crowd. That was one of the most intense situations I was in, but we didn't lose anyone.

It was really hard on Marcie. We e-mailed every day. I would call her every night, faithfully, unless I was out on a special mission or something. She didn't have to go too many days without hearing from me, but it was still nerve-wracking for her.

Then she got sick. She had fibrocystic breast disease, and it progressed really fast. She had been getting checkups every three months, but it got to the point where she only had 10% tumor-free tissue in each breast. She kept putting off the surgery to be there for her kids and to support me. The doctors in Pittsburgh told her it was pre-cancerous. They advised her to have bi-lateral mastectomies and then get breast implants — a form of reconstruction. A lot of people thought she was crazy, but she said, "I can't wait anymore. It's pre-cancerous now. The doctors said a year down the road I could get cancer, or it could be ten years. Why wait any longer?"

That was a big surgery, and I wanted to get leave to be with Marcie. But she said "No, you only have 14 days of leave. Spend that time with your kids." She kept saying I had enough stress, being in Iraq and fighting and trying to study at the same time. Still, I felt terrible that I couldn't be there for her.

That's why I put Marcie in for the "student support award" from Excelsior in 2010. She didn't know I had nominated her until she got the notice she had won. There I was in Iraq three times, and she helped me get through two of those, and through the bladder cancer, and then she went through a major surgery on her own. She chose to put her own needs aside to help me.

I was an operations sergeant pretty much the whole time I was in Iraq, and that was definitely stressful. Over the three and a half years I was there, I went on somewhere between 750 and 800 patrols into various cities. It took a toll on me. I was getting toward my retirement age and was thinking, *Man, I can't keep up with these young kids, wearing 85 pounds of gear.* I was in my late 30s, but when you're out there with 18-year-old kids, it's not easy. I knew I had to go back to school and get trained to do something else.

When I was introduced to Excelsior College at Fort Drum, I knew that I wanted to retire from the military. I wanted to be as successful in the civilian world as I had been in the military, but I had to acquire the education credentials to back that up. I was sure the experience as a military policeman would get me a good start, but I wanted to have more than a good start. I wanted to make good as a civilian. That's when I decided to pursue the Bachelor of Science in Criminal Justice, with the Law and Society emphasis.

Marcie always encouraged me to get my degree. I had been taking college classes all along, so I had a lot of credits. I started in 1990 in Germany, with the University of Maryland. However, the military didn't want to keep me anywhere longer than 24 months. My first duty assignment was Illinois, then I went to Germany, then to Fort Campbell, Kentucky, and then to Honduras, back to Fort Dix, on to Korea, then to Alabama, and Fort Hood, Texas, and back to Korea, and finally I got sent to Fort Drum. I stayed at Fort Drum the longest, because of the deployments to Iraq.

I kept taking college classes wherever I could — in-between deployments, in-between training exercises. I went to a community college in New Jersey; I went to a community college in Alabama. I got my associate's degree from Central Texas College, going to night school when I was at Fort Hood.

These classes were all time-and-place specific, and that was really hard. I'd work all day and then I'd have to travel to class, two or three times a week. This was right before online learning started. I think a lot of people are confused about the online learning format.

They'll ask me, "You got your college degree from a virtual class-room?" Well, you can go to Penn State and do all your classes online, and your degree is still from Penn State. You can go to Excelsior College, and it's the same degree—it's the same accreditation—and I think a lot of people don't understand that.

When I was in Iraq, going out on missions, coming back and studying was one of the things that helped me keep my sanity. Just being able to have that focus and knowing I was heading toward something positive was very important for me. And the professors were so encouraging. There were a couple of classes I had to take over again, not because I failed or anything, but because I literally didn't have time to do the assignments. I would have to ask for an extension, and they would say, "Hey, we get it. We know you're in Iraq. Stay safe." And they would give me an extension and I would get the course done. They worked with me really well throughout the whole program.

It was a challenge the whole way, but the professors gave me the drive to keep going. The years I was deployed, they knew how hard it was, and no one ever said to me, "You don't have your assignment completed. Forget it; you're done. You get zero." I was really impressed with their flexibility and their understanding of the uniqueness involved in trying to get an education while you're in the Army. To top it off, I earned a 3.45 GPA.

Now I'm working for the federal government. I work at an appeals court for Social Security disability. It worked out perfectly with my degree in Law and Society. I know I wouldn't have gotten this job without my degree. Now I'm also working on a Master's Degree in Organizational Management. I'm actually about halfway through it.

Marcie was so proud. She kept pushing and encouraging me the whole time because of everything I had gone through—working hard, never having anything, and trying to better myself by joining the Army. "You can do it," she'd tell me. "You'll be the first person in your family to achieve a college education." And she was right.

–4–

Meeting the Needs
of Adult Learners

Dan's varied educational experiences are similar to those of many adult learners, for whom life provides numerous challenges and distractions. His high school experience was far from rewarding—he didn't apply himself and was never held accountable for his actions. Like him, others have had such a poor time in high school that they question their own worth and wonder if they're college material.

In one of his *New York Times* columns in November 2010, Thomas L. Friedman points out that many young people are now so distracted by texting and other electronic multitasking that their school grades suffer, and consistently poor grades often precede the decision to drop out. Friedman then presents an even more serious problem: "Then, just as the world was getting flattened by globalization, technology went on a rampage—destroying more low-end jobs and creating more high-end jobs faster than ever. What computers, hand-held devices, wireless technology and robots do in aggregate is empower better-educated and higher-skilled workers to be more productive—so they can raise their incomes—while eliminating many lower-skilled service and factory jobs altogether. Now the best-educated workers, capable of doing the critical thinking that machines can't do, get richer, while the least-educated get 'pink slips.'"

This fits ominously with what US Secretary of Education Arne Duncan has warned about teens who flunk out or give up on high school: "When kids drop out today, they're condemned to poverty and social failure."

If fewer and fewer jobs will be generated in the future for those with only a high school diploma, then postsecondary education becomes one of the primary means of remaining competitive in the workplace and achieving at least a middle-class lifestyle. So for many working adults, earning a GED becomes the first step on the ladder.

In "Working Learners," Louis Soares highlights the diversity of his potential pool of working learners, but concedes that the diversity belies three key commonalities for adults who want to earn a postsecondary degree:

- To obtain a postsecondary education, students will most likely need to work and learn at the same time, or move frequently between the two.
- Because working learners are already in the workforce, they are seeking to build skills and credentials that employers will recognize and compensate.
- To be successful in college-level courses, working learners will need developmental education to shore up literacy, numeracy, technology, English-language skills, and college-success skills.

For many adults who already have their high school diplomas, jobs or military careers take precedence in their lives, and when they decide to return and study for a postsecondary degree, they need help getting up to speed.

Mike Rose, in his book *Why School? Reclaiming Education for All of Us*, echoes the findings of Soares and writes eloquently about remediation. He reminds us that in our open society, colleges shouldn't set themselves apart from their obligation to participate in a rich system of human development. Since many students don't arrive at college prepared for the rigors of higher education, our institutions must offer the guidance and training that will help ensure success: "This notion of a second chance, of building safety nets into a flawed system, fits with a democratic and humane definition of the person, one that offers a robust idea of development: the person as changing, coming at something again, fluid, living in a system that acknowledges that people change, retool, grow, need to return to old mistakes, or just to that which is past and forgotten."

Rose goes on to chronicle a 12-week crash course in college preparation for soldiers returning from Iraq and Afghanistan called "The Veterans Special Education Program." While the primary emphasis of the course was to provide essential remediation so the veterans could hit the ground running when they entered college courses, Rose reveals that "what the classroom full of veterans wanted most was, as one of them put it, 'to help our families understand what we went through.'. . . Our newest generation of veterans is returning to a warmer welcome than those who served in Vietnam, but the kind of war these veterans fought is similar, and their needs are as great. By one count, over 33,000 are injured, some severely. Others are or will be torn apart by psychological trauma. And many others will experience terrible distress as they try to find their way with family and community, with the economy and education."

Between these poles—the pragmatic desire to possess a high school diploma or GED so that enrollment in college is possible and the emotional/psychological/spiritual need that some people have to be understood by their loved ones—exists a broad spectrum of other needs that are just as important.

To better understand the needs of adult learners, The Lumina Foundation's Emerging Pathways Project studied the work of University of California, Riverside researcher John S. Levin, who has developed an adult learner typology—a continuum of adult and post-traditional learner characteristics—that can help education providers identify the degree to which a particular adult learner may be at risk of failing in a postsecondary school:

Nontraditional Students	Characteristics
Minimal Risk	One characteristic of nontraditional status, such as identity as an underrepresented minority or delayed college enrollment.
Moderate Risk	Two or three characteristics: underrepresented minority, or a person in need of financial aid, or a re-entry student.
High Risk	Many characteristics: minority, re-entry status, financial need, employed more than 20 hours a week, single parent.
Ultra-high Risk	Many characteristics, as above, as well as participation in programs outside the higher-education mainstream (non-credit continuing education courses; contract training provided by employers; for-credit continuing education courses). All these tend to place students on the periphery of higher education.

Higher-risk students, with limited governmental and institutional support, often drop in and out of postsecondary programs, earning so few credits that they are seldom acknowledged in formal accounting of student enrollments. In effect, they become invisible and, more often than not, become so discouraged that they give up on postsecondary achievement entirely. Lumina's report on this, "Returning to Learning," reveals that "The evidence gathered in the Emerging Pathways project suggests that although institutions are becoming sensitive to the challenges adult learners face, institutional actions and strategies are neither generally systematic nor empirically based. They do not account for the diverse identities, characteristics, and needs of the adult learner population."

So how can institutions change to meet the needs of working students? Lumina's project recommends these major actions:

- Develop pre-baccalaureate, career-related certificate programs that incorporate academic credit that can be counted toward a degree.
- Provide part-time degree programs.
- Create year-round, accelerated, and convenient programming.
- Facilitate degree mapping.
- To accommodate the intermittent enrollment patterns of many adult learners, financial support for less-than-half-time and intermittent enrollment must be available.
- Courses should be made available to fit the daily routines of adult learners. Convenience is crucial.

As we said in an earlier chapter, Arthur Levine believes that adult learners want convenience, good service, and financial aid. In other words, they want quality instruction at low cost, delivered with respect, and in ways that fit their busy schedules. These are the very things that the colleges profiled in this book already provide.

George Pruitt, president of Thomas Edison State College in Trenton, New Jersey, says the two principal characteristics of adult learners are the access barriers they face and the prior learning they possess: "Self-directed adult students can't put their careers, jobs, and families on hold to go sit in a classroom somewhere on Monday, Wednesday, and Friday. Today, most college students are over the age of 25 and going part-time. So it's a problem with governments at the state and federal levels that want to have a policy apparatus which assumes a reality that hasn't existed in 40 years. The other problem is the cost of higher education continues to go up. Getting adequate resources is a challenge.

"Moreover, their learning is continuous, and many of them have accumulated or achieved college-level capacities and competencies in non-collegiate environments. It doesn't make sense to have someone who is part of the Million-Dollar-Roundtable with Prudential Insurance Company, who teaches the state licensure exam and gained his knowledge of insurance from the industry itself, go back and take all the courses necessary to earn a degree in insurance. So one of the challenges then becomes, how do you acknowledge and evaluate college-level learning that was acquired in an extra-collegiate environment, and how do you acknowledge it with appropriate credit if the person can demonstrate that the competencies are there?

"To work on that problem, ten institutions came together to deal with the question of whether you could, in some valid and reliable way, assess college-level learning that was acquired outside of the classroom. Then the question became: If you can do that, can you find high-quality mechanisms for awarding college credit? The answer to that was yes, and out of that came portfolio assessment. The College Board was involved, and CLEP came out of that, and the whole prior learning assessment movement was born."

Ed Klonoski, president of Charter Oak State College in New Britain, Connecticut, echoes George Pruitt's comments about access, but he also offers distance learning as an important option for the asynchronous learning that adult students need: "The schedules that most higher education institutions offer for on-ground learning just don't fit an adult lifestyle—you've got a family; you've got a job; how are you going to fit a 4 o'clock Tuesday/Thursday into that? You can't.

"I'll tell you my favorite story. I used to run the Distance Learning Consortium in Connecticut. We did all the reviews, and we asked students how we were doing. Early on, this woman wrote back and said, 'I took my first online course this semester. Worst course I ever took. I've signed up for two more next semester.' It was about access.

"In the case of Charter Oak, when I came on the scene about twelve years ago, we started to explore distance learning. We were seeing distance learning courses on transcripts from other states, but Connecticut wasn't doing much back then. At that time, we weren't an instructional provider. We put some courses online, but we were just doing it because the adults needed the option and we were sort of filling gaps. Well, we went from filling gaps to being a major-league online provider, because our students choose that option. All the other options are still there—they do portfolios and they do testing—but they predominantly take online courses, and they take them from us."

Robert Mendenhall, president of Western Governors University in Salt Lake City, Utah, explains that WGU was created in 1997 by nineteen Western governors, in states from Indiana to Hawaii, to meet the needs of rural students who didn't have access to traditional higher education: "But it turns out that access is just as big an issue for an adult who is working full-time and, frankly, the local university doesn't usually offer a lot of classes that meet at 10 o'clock at night."

Even more than Charter Oak, WGU is entirely online, and Mendenhall stresses that his school is different than other online schools: "Traditional online education is basically a professor teaching a class. There are now two million courses on the Internet. So there's no need for us to go try to develop our own and claim they're the best. Instead, we have our faculty go find the best available courses, and we acquire the rights to use them with our students. In our case, we're really using the computer to do the teaching, to deliver the content, so our faculty do not develop or teach courses.

"I think traditional public and private institutions are generally effective in preparing Americans to compete, but only a privileged group of Americans—only those who can afford to send their kids to residential schools for four years or, in more cases, six years, to gain a degree. We're leaving out a bigger and bigger swath of America. The graduation rates are much lower for minority students, and for low-income students. The risk is that we get a completely bifurcated society, and I think that has negative social and economic implications for America. We simply have to provide less expensive, more flexible education for those who are not accessing higher education, both working adults and those who will become working adults in the future."

Alan Davis, president of Empire State College, which is perhaps the most unusual of the 64 institutions in the sprawling State University of New York (SUNY) system, admits that Empire State's relationship within SUNY is complicated: "I try very hard, working with SUNY, to actually differentiate us within the system. We were originally established to be a game-changer—to expand the scope and the reach of SUNY statewide—and so we were never supposed to be lumped in as just another state college.

"Excelsior and Empire State were born at exactly the same time, in 1971, in parallel. They shared some of the same initial Ford Foundation funding, and they were established for the same reason—to fill the enormous gap in the higher education system for those wanting to return to education."

Empire State bridges that gap by offering adult students one-on-one mentoring at 35 locations throughout New York State. This mentoring model, coupled with a more self-directed curriculum and a basically open enrollment process, adds to their unique status within the SUNY system. Davis sees all three elements as essential antidotes to a national higher education system that is increasing class disparity: "The gap is widening. We like to think that education is the great leveler, but it's not. We're doing more and more wonderful things to enrich the learning experiences of people who are already destined to succeed. That is, they come from families with good incomes; they're raised by parents who have been educated; they've been supported in all kinds of ways through their different schools; they're on track and they'll do well; and traditional universities do a great job of taking them to the next level and setting them on the path to success.

"For people who don't have all those advantages, it's a different story, and their degree attainment, while it is going up, generally, across the board, it's not going up nearly as fast as their more privileged counterparts. So there is a gap and you worry that there is going to be more and more demand from people who missed out, who want to come back, who need to come back, and I can see the role of the alternative and adult-serving institutions increasing substantially over the next few years."

Thomas Edison, Charter Oak, Western Governors, and Empire State College—the colleges that we include here because they each serve adult learners well and share some of Excelsior's education methods—clearly have their own ways of meeting Arthur Levine's requirements for convenience and respect. Prior learning assessment honors the training and experience that most students possess when they return to school and gives them credit; online courses offer adult students the ability to study whenever their schedules permit; and mentoring programs provide one-on-one guidance that can ensure the continuous support that many returning students need for success.

Excelsior College, like its "sister" institutions, was created to help self-motivated people earn degrees and achieve their dreams. The reason for the creation of Excelsior (formerly Regents) in 1971 was, as Alan Davis stated above, to serve working adults—people who had not, by virtue of life's circumstances, been able to complete a traditional degree. Initially, Excelsior reviewed what adult students already had accomplished, determined what was needed, and then advised them about where to study and how to do that in a way that met both their academic and financial capabilities. Increasingly, its students, who were arriving with varied backgrounds, objected to the idea of being sent to another institution or, in some cases multiple ones, to finish their requirements. They wanted to do everything with one institution.

Thus, Excelsior made the decision in 2003 to start offering instruction, and over the last seven years, that has become the biggest piece of its business. The college sees more revenue today from instruction than from its credit aggregation and prior learning assessment. Once students have established a comfortable relationship with a person who treats them with respect, offers intelligent guidance, and understands their specific needs—whether it's an instructor, mentor, or advisor—they don't want to build such relationships all over again in another place just for a course or two.

The five colleges named here have been knocking down barriers to access for working students. They've eliminated the barrier of time with asynchronous programs that are not time-and-place specific. They've removed the barrier of distance by using the Internet to deliver online programs. They don't ask people to repeat courses or areas in which they've already developed competency just to satisfy requirements.

Excelsior sees itself as unique in terms of the number of its advisors: 40 divided between four schools. This is substantially different than in traditional higher education, particularly because of the advising conducted on the front end. While using technology to a great degree, the college offers every single person a handcrafted, individually prepared learning plan. Excelsior's students know exactly which aspects of their prior learning will apply toward their degree and which will not. Once their performance is assessed, they receive a detailed map of how to work toward their degrees.

Adult educators report that many people who return to school become straight-A students. Even though their previous transcripts may not predict such excellent performance, adult students often become intensely motivated. Frequently, 20 years or more may have passed since they were last in school, but with individual support, they can develop the self-confidence necessary to get them through their first two or three courses. After that, they get it, and they push themselves to succeed.

– 5 –

John Ebersole: Educating a College President

The traditional image of a college president is a high achiever in high school who breezes through undergraduate and graduate school to land a job as a teacher and then administrator at a prestigious institute of higher education. But Excelsior College's president, John Ebersole, has much more in common with his uncommon students, who may see something of their own struggles in his lifelong pursuit of learning.

As a farm boy growing up near Windsor, Missouri, my first eight years of education were spent at "Sunnyside," a one-room country school with outdoor toilets and a stable for students' horses, although none of us owned a horse during my time there. One teacher taught all subjects for all eight grades. However, with about a dozen students, on average, some grades had no students. In retrospect, I can see that the opportunity to observe and listen to the instruction given to those in more advanced grades was an advantage, as was the repetition that came later. In fact, the instruction followed closely the old adage about effective public speaking: tell them what you're going to tell them, then tell them, and then tell them what you told them. After multiple exposures to the material—which was literally reading, writing and arithmetic—even the slowest students developed a fairly strong understanding of the basics.

Windsor was a rural community with about 2,500 inhabitants, 80 miles southwest of Kansas City. Its primary claim to fame was that it was a gateway to the Lake of the Ozarks. Windsor was also home to an International Shoe Company manufacturing plant, the area's largest employer. That was where my mother worked. The summer before I started high school, my father passed away after many years of recurring illness. Our "farm" was not really big enough to support us, and my mom's paycheck from her factory job, where she sewed all manner of footwear, was $60 a week. It became pretty clear that I needed to take on after-school and summer jobs to bolster our income.

Windsor High School served approximately 200 students, many of whom were from the Air Force families that dotted the countryside around nearby Whiteman Air Force Base, which was both a SAC bomber and a Nike missile facility. Thanks to a large yellow bus, the eight-mile commute from our home to the high school was covered in under an hour, each way. The two hours of round-trip transit involved the pickup and return of nearly 20 students from along narrow gravel roads and lanes that surrounded the town. While I no longer recall the number of students in my freshman class, there were 40 graduating seniors—quite an increase from the three who moved up from Sunnyside Elementary in 1958.

I received good grades during my first two years of high school, but these plummeted when I turned 16, purchased a 1931 Model A coupe for $200, and discovered girls. My job at the local newspaper, *The Windsor Review*, had to do triple duty: help out with home expenses, buy gas for the car—luckily only 35 cents a gallon then—and support my burgeoning social life.

While I was active in sports, student government, the school newspaper, and band, I found schoolwork less interesting. I ranked academics well below work, dating, and extracurricular activities, and as a result, my GPA fell to the point where I was required to take an extra course to graduate: Senior English.

The night before the final exam in Senior English — the exam that would pretty much determine if I would graduate — the newspaper printing press broke. To make the time-consuming repairs and complete the press run for the next day's edition, I had to work all night. As I entered the classroom the next morning, bleary-eyed and unprepared, I asked myself, *How did I get to this point? Why does my very ability to graduate from high school now depend upon my performance during the next hour? How did I let my grades slip from the As and Bs of my early years to my current Cs and Ds?*

It was true that during the preceding four years I had sampled much of what my small high school had to offer. As a freshman and sophomore, I took Shop (learning to weld) and Agriculture (learning to judge meat quality), played football (but not well), ran track, and was "chaplain" of the Future Farmers of America Chapter. Additionally, despite not being able to read a note of music, I played in the percussion section of the school band. I was a very flashy cymbal player, but only a mediocre snare drummer.

In my junior year, things changed. An unwelcome stepfather entered my life. His arrival brought tension into our house, and the ensuing conflicts made it easier to stay away from home more often. Moreover, after three years of working outside school and adding my income to my mom's, I did not take well to being replaced as the man of the house. While still active in a range of extracurricular activities, my relationships with friends took on a new, more urgent importance. I needed my friends to become an extended family, and that extended family grew quickly. I had developed solid friendships with not only the "hoods," who smoked, got poor grades, and existed at the fringe of the school's social life, but also the "ins," who were popular, achieved better grades, and were envied role models, at least in the eyes of most parents.

No longer feeling supported at home, I let the importance of my friends exceed whatever approval might have come with continued good grades. Also, I still needed to earn a paycheck, and such activities as the school paper (where I was the editor) and Student Council (where I was president), took additional time away from class work.

So, upon reflection, I knew how I had ended up in that fix. I sat down to take the critical exam at 8 a.m., and an hour later my English teacher, Ms. Tara Kidwell, shook me awake and retrieved my unmarked exam book. I was convinced, of course, that I would be in Windsor for another year. Not until some days later did she summon me to an after-class meeting to tell me that, based on my earlier, stronger work, she was giving me a passing grade—a gift that allowed me to graduate. I still feel grateful for her compassion.

While Ms. Kidwell will always be counted among those who made a difference in my education and my life, graduating from high school certainly didn't open any doors. I had neither the money nor the grades to go to college, as most of my friends were doing. Local employment was equally discouraging. I had worked one summer for International Shoe and another for Moss Pontoons, the two largest employers in the community. In the first instance, I had felt like a mere appendage of a machine, and in the second, I learned that I am *extremely* allergic to fiberglass.

Even though I had been active in both 4H and Future Farmers of America, the prospect of a lifetime of building fences, milking cows, and doing the typical work of a farmer held zero appeal. Thus, I found myself with but a single option. Like so many others, I decided that my only route of escape started at the front door of the local military recruiter. On June 30, 1962, I became only the second citizen of Johnson County, Missouri, to enlist in the US Coast Guard. My predecessor had joined 44 years earlier during World War I.

Following recruit training in Alameda, California, in the midst of the Cuban Missile Crisis, I was dispatched to the Coast Guard

Training Center in Groton, Connecticut, to become an electronics technician. My test scores at the time of recruitment had suggested that I was a likely candidate for one of the service's more academically demanding specialties. Two weeks into that difficult curriculum, though, the school's instructors and I agreed that this was not to be. I had spent a few too many hours sleeping through high school algebra.

It was not until the winter of 1964 that I started to see some connection between education, personal growth, and earnings. Having gone to sea following my rude awakening in electronics school, I became an apprentice yeoman—an administrative clerk who obtained the needed specialty knowledge on-the-job rather than by attending a formal school. Using correspondence courses to prepare for advancement exams, I found that I did quite well, moving from enlisted pay grade E-3 to E-4 in a single attempt.

However, the cost of my success was that I had to give up the comfort of my afloat office, which had been my reward for learning how to type, and accept transfer to a damp, dank Coast Guard Air Station on Annette Island, Alaska, off Ketchikan. During this period, I had also become a husband and a father, but the new deployment and my junior E4 status wouldn't allow me to be accompanied by my wife and new daughter.

Air Station Annette was essentially a flying ambulance service for Southeastern Alaska. It flew those in need of advanced medical care not available locally to either Seattle or Anchorage. The usual clientele included victims of drunken brawls, knife fights, hunting and logging accidents, fishing boat injuries, and even an occasional car wreck. In addition, there were the cases of the native Alaskans who poisoned themselves drinking various substitutes for alcohol. I shall never forget the very large Indian woman that we had to place in a straightjacket as she battled demons brought on by a binge with Sterno and rubbing alcohol.

Annette's weather in 1964 included 170 inches of rain and more than 50 inches of snow. That extreme weather was a primary cause of stress. On those few occasions when the sun did come out, the station would declare a holiday, regardless of the day of the week. Unfortunately, such days were few and far between. That unrelenting gloom and isolation pushed many locals, as well as some Coast Guard personnel, over the edge. I became all too familiar with incidents of spousal abuse, alcoholism, and even suicide. I would later think that I saw more death and suffering firsthand in my year in Alaska than during my year of combat in Vietnam.

For me, Annette offered the solitude I needed to learn. I continued to move up through the ranks, passing two more promotion exams. And it was there that I also started taking correspondence courses for college credit from the US Armed Forces Institute at the University of Wisconsin.

The following year, I was assigned to the staff of the captain of the port in Mobile, Alabama. During this assignment, my wife and I had our second daughter, and I began to consider the Coast Guard as a career. I also realized that acquiring more education could help open options for me within the service, including the possibility of officer candidate school. Three years out of high school, married with two children, I enrolled in my first-ever face-to-face college course—Introduction to Political Science—offered through the evening division of the University of South Alabama, which was at that point a brand new school with a single building. It did not go well.

I am not sure if my difficulty with this course came from my lack of confidence as a student, the challenge of the work, coping with a brand new baby, or the fact that I was treated to a full-blown case of chicken pox by my eldest daughter during the academic term. With angry pox sprouting on the soles of my feet, in my ears and hair, and even crusted in my eyelids, I retreated to a bathtub full of oatmeal to get relief from the unbearable itching. As you can imagine, this did not lend itself to retaining much of the required reading. All in all, I felt lucky when I received a C; however, I also felt no burning desire to repeat the experience.

Instead of taking a second college course, I found myself heading for officer candidate school in the fall of 1966. My advancement to pay grade E-6, as well as four years of active service, qualified me for entry to OCS, at a time when the Coast Guard needed additional officers to man not only the ice breakers it was taking over from the Navy, but also the patrol boats it was sending to Vietnam. Officer candidate school, with its mix of classroom and hands-on training, provided an opportunity for me to learn a number of academic subjects and apply what I had learned. This included the use of various quantitative concepts to celestial navigation, piloting, seamanship, and marine engineering. I quickly learned that there was a connection between physics and geometry and how you handle a ship, and that oceanography and meteorology involved more than a little science. More importantly, perhaps, was that I had graduated second out of a class of 248, which gave me a much-needed boost of self-confidence. It also made me think that going back to school wouldn't be so difficult, after all.

My first assignment as an officer was aboard the cutter *Chilula*, a former Navy fleet tug with a crew of 80. While my primary responsibility was as the ship's communications officer, I was also given the collateral assignment of education officer. In this latter role, I was responsible for helping to motivate others to take both professional and academic courses, as well as College Level Examination Program (CLEP) exams. The importance of this work was driven home by the ship's captain, Jim Randle, who took a personal interest in the growth and development of both the officers and crew, making it a goal for all officers to help get their subordinates promoted. It was here, finally, that the seeds of my future commitment to education were sown. While by then I clearly understood the connection between learning and career opportunity, my own education had to wait a bit longer while I completed two more assignments afloat.

My first command was the *Cape Morgan*, ported at the "Old Rice Mill" in Charleston, South Carolina. She spent much of her time in the Florida Keys, picking up Cuban refugees along the Cay

Sal Bank between Cuba and the United States. Our work was focused entirely on search and rescue.

My second command, in Vietnam, offered an incredibly intense and challenging professional testing ground. My vessel, the *Point Grace*, was a former search and rescue cutter, but it had been newly outfitted with multiple weapons and a coat of the US Navy's finest battleship-gray paint. Home ported in Cat Lo at the mouth of the Saigon River, *Point Grace* had been sent to Vietnam three years earlier as part of Operation Market Time, a naval blockade of the South's coastline.

By the time I arrived in the summer of 1969, her mission had changed. As a result of the blockade's success, the North was forced to create an inland supply line — the Ho Chi Minh Trail — running along the borders of Laos and Cambodia. This caused the Navy to change its strategy in the South. Instead of patrolling off shore and looking for the occasional blockade runner, *Grace's* shallow draft allowed her to navigate the rivers and canals of the Mekong Delta. Our mission was to intercept men and materials being sent down the various rivers from the Cambodian border. But we also launched and recovered small boats at night in heavy seas, went alongside much larger vessels to obtain water and supplies, fired support for US and Vietnamese units ashore, and searched hundreds of sampans a week. For me, the responsibilities that came with these activities were both challenging and rewarding. Each assignment, whether inserting Navy Seals, covering Army sweeps, or creating ambush sites for clandestine Viet Cong, carried the potential for life and death decisions. That was heady stuff for a 24-year-old former farm boy.

As I think back over my time in Vietnam, I still regard it as a period of tremendous personal growth and learning, where I met and passed the various challenges placed before me. I was also proud that while we were one of the more aggressive boats in the division, we were also careful about the fights we got into. Even though we were damaged in one enemy ambush to the point of needing repairs

600 miles away in Singapore, none of my crew was lost or even seriously injured. All of us came home.

As for practical education, it's clear to me that my understanding of leadership, motivation, decision making, risk analysis, behavior under stress, morality, and strategy were all enhanced. But, most importantly, I learned a great deal about myself.

Upon returning from Vietnam in the summer of 1970, I was assigned to head the training branch of a new division within Coast Guard Headquarters in Washington, DC. With no prior background, I was asked to develop training programs in marine law enforcement for Coast Guard and uniformed marine police officers from various states. I was also expected to create and disseminate boating safety materials to the general public. To acquire the basic knowledge and skills for my new job, I spent one summer at the University of Wisconsin in Madison, learning about adult learning theory, then the next at the University of Indiana in Bloomington, studying methods of instruction. The more I learned, the more I wanted to earn a degree myself. Of course, I didn't realize then that the educational experiences the Coast Guard was providing would build the foundation for a later career.

During this time in Washington, my wife and I both enrolled in the University of Virginia's degree-completion program at Ft. Belvoir. During the next three years, we took two to three courses per term, year-round, spending more money on babysitting than on tuition. However, before completing the program, I found myself returning to sea. Not until two years later was I able to go back to class.

In 1977, while serving as the director of the Coast Guard Auxiliary in Long Beach, California, I heard that Pacific Western University could award a degree based upon "life experience and prior academic work." After going through their assessment process and paying $1,200, I was awarded a bachelor's degree. However, a year later, I learned about the significance of regional accreditation. Pacific Western was not so accredited, and their "degree" was worthless.

My disappointment at being misled and paying for a bogus diploma was offset by the news that I had been selected to attend the Naval War College (NWC) at Newport, Rhode Island, commencing in the fall of 1978. Knowing that an undergraduate degree was normally expected, though not required, of those attending, I enrolled at Long Beach Community College to take a series of courses that I felt would help prepare me for the War College experience.

Some years earlier, NWC graduates who completed two additional courses were awarded a master's degree by George Washington University. But during Vice Admiral Stansfield Turner's tenure as college president, he made the program more rigorous but terminated the relationship with GWU, resulting in a far-more-demanding program that no longer resulted in the award of an academic degree. Vice Admiral Jim Stockdale, who was president during my time at NWC, retained that model. So despite my having been designated a "distinguished graduate" of the War College and having earned a GPA of 3.75, I received no degree. It was not until years later that NWC obtained regional accreditation and the ability to award its own graduate degrees.

With decades of experience, much ACE-reviewed military training, multiple course completions, both through correspondence courses and in classrooms, completion of a yearlong graduate program, and a total credit count approaching 180 semester units, I arrived at John F. Kennedy University in Orinda, California, in the fall of 1979, seeking to complete my undergraduate degree. JFKU had been established in 1964 specifically to meet the needs of working adult students. Unfortunately, it also had a residency requirement: they expected 30 of the final credits to be earned "in residence."

Recognizing my success at the Naval War College, JFKU agreed to conditionally admit me to their master's program. All I had to do was satisfy course and degree requirements, including class attendance. That would prove to be a challenge. As commanding officer of the Coast Guard's Pacific Area Training Team, I found myself traveling 36 weeks per year—from Kodiak to San Diego,

San Francisco to Guam, and all coastal ports in between. Thanks to some very creative travel planning and a supportive boss, I was able to make it work. In June 1982, twenty years after graduating from high school, I was awarded my first postsecondary credential, a Master of Public Administration, along with the Morrison Award for the highest GPA in the program.

During the two decades between graduations, I had married, helped to raise three children, spent six tours at sea, gone to war, and moved seventeen times. I also had completed nearly half again as much academic work as is typically required for an undergraduate degree, all at the expense of the US Coast Guard and the taxpayers.

Had I known about the founding of Regents College in 1971, I might have taken advantage of its ability to aggregate all of my many sources of academic credit, ACE-reviewed military training, transfer courses, and exam performance, and then compared all of that against various degree requirements. With Regents' guidance, and its ability to accept 100% of my degree requirements in transfer, I might even have earned an undergraduate degree.

–6–

Which Schools
Offer What?

Our profiled students have demonstrated self-direction, persistence, compassion, and courage throughout their careers. Those qualities have figured prominently in the ways they achieved success. They relied upon themselves, and they never stopped trying to make a difference for other people. The fact that each has encountered difficulties with traditional institutions may furnish some of the explanation for the current educational crisis we face.

As former President Bill Clinton said in a recent address at the University at Albany, the problem in wealthier, developed countries like the United States is stagnation: "At some point, people get more interested in what they have in the present than in creating the future." If that is an accurate perception, then we have to make a realistic appraisal of whether it's true for each one of us. Have we become complacent? Are we comfortable with seeing our incomes diminish and our country fall economically behind China or India or other countries that work harder than we do? Do we have the courage that previous generations of Americans have shown? The time to answer those questions is now because, given the speed at which technology is reshaping our world, what we predict for the future will arrive faster than ever before.

If you are a working adult and have already made the decision to return to school, and you're ready to pursue postsecondary education and earn a degree, what are your best options? Over the next several pages, we will examine the various sectors of higher education. With more than 4,000 regionally accredited institutions in the United States, it is not possible to describe all the options. Instead we will profile Excelsior College, Thomas Edison State College, Charter Oak State College, Western Governors University, and Empire State College—five schools that are focused exclusively on the needs of the adult learner. Each of these is regionally accredited, not-for-profit, and well established.

In addition, there are divisions of traditional colleges and universities that serve adults. These are usually titled as continuing, extended, or professional education units. Furthermore, many for-profit universities also target adults. This latter group has recently received a great deal of negative attention from Congress and the Department of Education. The issues have centered on misrepresentation, student debt from federal financial aid, and corner-cutting in regard to hours of instruction. The important thing to know about these schools is that only a fraction of them were involved in the type of abuse alleged. Most of the larger and better-known for-profit institutions are doing a good job of delivering quality education. As we point out later in the book, these institutions are attuned to the needs of the adult learner but tend to be more expensive than their not-for-profit counterparts.

Let's look at the different types of institutions that comprise American higher education:

Community Colleges

These publicly funded two-year institutions are great places for a cost-conscious student to satisfy general education requirements that are a part of any undergraduate degree. They tend to be low cost, and most will have agreements with the public four-year institutions of their state, which assures that credits you earn will be accepted as having fulfilled requirements for a bachelor's degree. These colleges cater to students of all ages, and they can provide a range of counseling services that are as important to an adult student as to younger ones.

Four-Year Public Colleges and Universities

While only a small percentage of students complete college in four years anymore, we still use this terminology in distinguishing between public "teaching" institutions and the larger, public "research" universities. Both will typically offer bachelor's and master's degrees, but research doctorates (PhDs) are usually only offered by research-focused institutions. As you will find in the world of higher education, few hard and fast rules apply, and there are exceptions to almost any categorization we offer. The public, four-year, teaching institution is where most American students receive their educations. These colleges and universities are usually less expensive and more liberal in their admission policies than private schools or research universities. They also tend to be large and more focused on the traditional-aged than the adult student.

Public Research Universities

These tend to be known as the "flagship" or "land-grant" institutions in a state—the former term meaning that they are, at least in part, tax-funded, prestigious, and selective in their admissions. The latter term refers to the means by which they were created. In the second half of the nineteenth century, the federal government designated and provided land for such an institution in each state. In fact, both terms may refer to the same institution. While still less costly than many private colleges, this category of school tends to be very large and very selective in terms of undergraduate admissions. Nonetheless, this could be an option for those seeking a "brand name" at a reasonable cost. The trade-off comes with the potential difficulty in gaining admission, and with the fact that such institutions tend to be the least adult-friendly, at least at the undergraduate level. Most do not even offer a part-time program for those who are working.

Institutes

Some academic institutions use neither the term "college" nor "university." These tend to be very specialized schools and are predominately found in such fields as art, engineering, or some specific occupational area. These may be either public or private in terms of their funding/support model.

Private Colleges and Universities

At one time, nearly all private colleges in America were religious in nature. Some of our best-known private universities were founded by churches, such as the Methodist involvement in the creation of Boston University, Duke, SMU, Vanderbilt, Northwestern, and the University of Southern California. Today those connections are no longer as close as they once were. The common factor with most private institutions is that they receive no direct support in the form of tax dollars. They must support themselves based upon tuition, grants, and giving. As a result, they tend to be more expensive than public institutions. Schools in this category range from very small liberal arts schools to major research universities, such as Harvard and Stanford. Some are selective in admissions while others are less so, depending upon the stated mission of the school. Cost and quality can vary widely with these institutions, as with any of the others mentioned.

For-Profit Universities

All of the nationally serving for-profits use the term "university." This is intended to convey an image of substance, breadth, and stability. It also helps with recruitment, as the term "college" conveys a smaller, more limited type of institution—a perception that is not always accurate. These institutions, which are accountable to owners or shareholders, have profits as their primary mission. They make money through the delivery of instruction and credentials to students, both traditional-aged and adult. These schools tend to offer a high level of customer service and convenience. They also provide a variety of study options and are focused on meeting the needs of the adult student. Thus, instruction is delivered online, in evening classroom programs, or both.

Adult-Serving Institutions

The institutions that we profile here are those that specifically serve adults. Time and space limit this discussion to five truly unique adult-serving schools, as well as a handful of others that are more traditional in some ways but are also adult-focused. All of these are not-for-profit and are regionally accredited. They are also open enrollment, in that they believe that everyone should have the opportunity to demonstrate their abilities and to determine for themselves whether earning a degree is part of their future.

It is encouraging to note that research by the National Center for Public Policy in Higher Education has found that open-access colleges such as these are responsible for the greatest gains in graduation rates over the past decade. While critics might question the quality of graduates and their academic experience, these schools are able to point to learning-outcome assessments not found elsewhere. For example, Excelsior's Associate's Degree in Nursing program (the nation's largest, with more than 14,000 enrollments) requires satisfactory completion of a hands-on, clinical-skill competency assessment. No other associate's degree nursing program in the country has such an assessment of competency as a condition of graduation.

What we particularly want to emphasize is that the adult-serving schools profiled here are accredited by the same organizations that accredit the name-brand institutions. If you're thinking about getting a degree, those from Excelsior College, Charter Oak State College, Thomas Edison State College, Western Governors University, and Empire State College are degrees that you can build on.

President John Ebersole on Excelsior College

Inspired by the British Open University (OU) in the 1960s, the Regents of the State of New York created their own "open" institutions in 1971: Regents College and Empire State College. With funding from the Ford and Carnegie Foundations, Regents and Empire State became America's first external-degree providers. Like the OU, both were founded as open-enrollment, adult-focused institutions for those who had historically not been well served by more traditional forms of higher education. Anyone with a high school diploma or a GED was afforded admission. While contrary to the strategy of using greater student selectivity to achieve prestige, the open-enrollment philosophy has given many mid-career adults a second chance at earning a degree. It has also provided many minority students access to higher education and economic growth.

Accredited by the Middle States Commission on Higher Education since 1973, Regents offered no instruction until 25 years after its founding. Until then, students requiring coursework in order to complete a degree would typically be directed to other institutions after an assessment of their prior learning.

In 1998, the college was granted a charter as an independent, not-for-profit institution. A condition of the new status was that the college change its name to Excelsior (Latin for "ever upward" and the state's motto). Commencing in 2003, the college embraced online learning in addition to the independent-study formats used by its Associate's Degree in Nursing (ADN) program. Today, the majority of Excelsior's 30,000 students remain candidates for assessment, with approximately 8,000 students taking online courses exclusively. All graduate programs require online coursework.

Because of Excelsior's commitment to meeting students where they are, academically as well as geographically, the college has adopted a number of procedures and credit-earning methodologies not found at other institutions. The commitment and expertise of its advisors is often cited as one of Excelsior's greatest strengths. Despite the college's growing enrollment, advisors continue to create individual learning plans for each entering student. This requires combining and assessing prior learning experiences, as well as mapping different options for fulfilling outstanding requirements. Once the learning plan is in place, advisors continue to assist the student in ensuring the applicability of particular courses, whether from Excelsior or elsewhere. An appropriate analogy might be that advisors act as primary-care specialists who guide students through the degree-completion process much like a doctor might manage one's healthcare.

Under the external-degree model, students could transfer 100% of their degree work to Regents. Over the years, however, this policy has been modified to one of low residency whereby some coursework—information literacy and capstone assessments—is now required from the college.

Associate's and bachelor's degrees are earned through a methodology that aggregates credit from multiple sources and then assesses prior learning for degree applicability. It matches earned credits against degree requirements as set by the New York State Department of Education. Any areas of deficiency can be satisfied through one of five options: credit transferred from another institution, credit for relevant training, credit by examination, credit by assessment portfolio, or coursework at Excelsior.

Transfer credit: The typical Excelsior student presents an average of five transcripts upon application for admission. The college's advisors aggregate this credit, determine its fit to the degree sought, offer alternatives, if appropriate, and create a degree-completion plan. Older courses in fast-changing fields such as information technology often have to be refreshed. As required by the Middle States Commission on Higher Education (Excelsior's regional accreditor), criteria have been established for evaluating and accepting credit from nationally accredited institutions, as well. In the case of credit earned abroad, the college uses international transcript evaluation services to determine equivalencies.

Excelsior's liberal transfer policy enables its students to complete a degree without having to retake coursework previously completed with a passing grade. As a result, in 2009, the value of accepted transfer credit by the college was $185 million (using Excelsior's then undergraduate tuition rate of $315). This represents a tremendous savings of time and money to the student and, potentially, to employers and/or federal financial aid programs.

Credit for training: Excelsior recognizes credit recommendations from the American Council on Education (ACE) for prior military or corporate training. Additionally, the college's faculty may conduct assessments of instruction from non-academic sources when it has not been ACE reviewed. With funding from the US Department of Justice, the college has, for instance, reviewed and proposed credit recommendations for a number of government-supported law enforcement academies.

Through a combination of ACE credit recommendations and coursework at Excelsior or elsewhere, many active-duty military students find that they are able to complete a degree with little additional work. In 2009 Excelsior was designated as one of the top ten institutions serving the armed services.

Credit by examination: With attention from the Lumina Foundation and the Obama administration, institutions are rediscovering prior learning assessment as a means to accelerate degree completion and to reduce cost. At Excelsior, this process relies less on the portfolio method (which it does employ), than on its own battery of psychometrically validated examinations.

Regents College offered a credit-by-examination option to students shortly after its founding, drawing upon the Regents' resources and historic work of examining New York's graduating secondary students. Today, Excelsior offers some 50 subject examinations of its own, while also accepting credit from the College Board's CLEP Program and the DSST Program of the Educational Testing Service (ETS). With the philosophy that what you know is more important than where or how you learned it, Excelsior/Regents has been a leader in the learning-assessment field.

For those wishing to apply credit earned through examination toward a degree being earned elsewhere, Excelsior provides a transcript that reflects exam performance. Currently, some 1,500 institutions from across the country accept credit-by-exam toward their degree requirements.

Excelsior College Exams (ECE) are available to all and are administered on demand at Pearson/Vue testing centers worldwide. A unique aspect of the ECE Program is the prospective test takers' ability to take a practice exam prior to taking the one of record whose results are shown on a transcript. This allows prospective test takers to evaluate their readiness and to reduce the risk of having a "Failed" on their transcript. The cost of Excelsior's ECE assessments varies somewhat by subject area and number of credits awarded for passage. However, the cost per credit, including the practice exam and testing fee, is typically under $100 per unit of credit. More information about credit-by-exam is presented in Appendix C.

Credit by assessment: In addition to its exams, Excelsior uses other methods of evaluating learning and competency. They range from computer simulations to performance assessments in subject-specific settings, such as a hospital. Excelsior is in the process of creating outcome assessments for each of its major programs. As higher education moves into an era of increased accountability, such tools are expected to help measure both the success of the student and the effectiveness of the college.

Credit from instruction: For students who require instruction to complete a degree, the college offers more than 300 online courses. In 2009, it also offered its first face-to-face instruction—at the Army's Sergeant-Majors Academy in Ft. Bliss, Texas.

By assessing what has been previously learned and combining that with knowledge that can be obtained online, Excelsior believes it can ease the anxiety of returning to school after many years, while remaining affordable. Through the acceptance of previously earned credit, determinations of credit equivalency, and credit-by-examination, it can keep the cost of an academic credential below that of even a public institution, where a minimum number of credits have to be completed in residence, regardless of prior work. Furthermore, by offering year-round programs and compressed terms (whereby students complete two courses per term in an eight-week sequence rather than concurrently), Excelsior offers accelerated formats that enable students to move more quickly toward an income-enhancing credential.

President Ed Klonoski on Charter Oak State College

We started in 1973, and we were really invented because women were coming back to college after interrupting their collegiate experience to have husbands and families, and higher education really wasn't very welcoming. They were told they would have to start over because their credits were outdated. Traditional schools treated these experienced women, who had been running PTAs and all kinds of things, as if they were 18-year-old rookies. So Charter Oak State College was really invented to validate prior learning. And our student body is predominantly female—then and now.

We're 38 years old, so let's say for the first 25 years of our history, our students—just like at Excelsior—took their credits from everybody else and aggregated their degrees here. You could build portfolios for credit, and we encouraged it. You could do testing for credit. You could validate prior learning, for example, by bringing us ACE-recommended training experience, which we would also bless for credit. What we were really invented to do was to treat adults as if they might know something, and explore their work history to see if in fact they do have something that they could make a portfolio case for.

Students are now arriving here with fewer credits. We used to be specialists in the "100-credit wonder." Somebody who had gone to five or six different schools in over twenty years and had amassed all these undergraduate credits but no degree—we still solve that problem brilliantly. But now our students are showing up with 75 credits, and they're doing 85% of the rest of their work in our online courses. And they made that choice. I can't say that the college aimed for it. But we're certainly aiming to stay there.

Charter Oak got into distance learning just to fill gaps for their students, and the students liked it so much and the revenue from it was so positive that we are now an online college. What we do now is instruction. The 18-year-old population cohort is shrinking, and the adult population is expanding. We're good at reaching out to that population, because we've been doing it for 38 years.

Our average age at graduation is 41. But I want to trend that younger, because I think if you're 23 or 24 and don't have a bachelor's degree, you ought to know already that you have a problem. If you're not in a trade, you shouldn't wait until you're 35 to realize you need a bachelor's degree. You ought to know it sooner, and you ought to be using somebody like us to make progress toward that sooner. So I want to see my trend-line go down on age. You shouldn't have to wait until you're 50 years old before you get your credential.

Now I don't mind if you're 30. I don't mind if you come to me with work experience and a family. I prefer you as a student that way, because you come to me with an adult profile, which means you're probably pretty focused and driven, and you're a consumer. If I treat you badly, you'll leave. Traditional higher education can treat the 18-year-olds any way they want. They're captured, and don't have anywhere to go; they like the dorm; they like the social life; they're not going to leave. They don't have the same concierge-customer ethic that adult-serving institutions have to have. Adults know what they expect when they buy something.

We have one program: we just do degree completion at the associate's and bachelor's levels. We're about to launch our first master's degree. Our sister organization in Connecticut—The Distance Learning Consortium—has two virtual high schools so, in actuality, we offer high school through the bachelor's and soon through the master's. I think we're the only organization in the country that does that.

We have a little over 3,000 students. Because we do enrollment every day, it's hard to give you a completely accurate figure. We want to double that in the next five years, and we won't need more buildings to do that. We do it all online, so we don't need more classroom space. Architecture for us—the footprint—stays narrow.

Over a hundred adjuncts do our teaching, distributed all across the country, all the way out to Hawaii. They have to have at least a master's degree in their field, if not the full PhD, and it's nice if they have online teaching experience. Increasingly they do. Lots of our faculty are full-time someplace else and they're teaching on the side for us. We have a managing faculty, and they have to be full-time at a Connecticut two- or four-year institution. I'd say there are about 40 of them, and they create our academic policies.

An education at Charter Oak costs about $200 per credit, with three credits per course, or $600 a course. We have the lowest-cost bachelor's degree in the state, bar none. I mean, we're a state institution. We have a 25% subsidy from the state, but that's going down. We take great pride in being a low-cost provider. And I actually think, from a marketing standpoint, that as distance learning gets bigger, we're not a bad place to be. Phoenix is three times the cost of us—$600 a credit unit—and you need 120 credits, give or take an inch.

The real question is: How many credits do you have when you walk in the door, and how many more do you need? As I said earlier, that's trending down. Students are coming in with fewer credits. We're also seeing more students come in to get their associate's degree from us. We're even seeing associate's students who almost always finish the bachelor's with us. So we're being used in some new ways, because distance learning is empowering people.

Our mission has always been adults, degree completion, and post-traditional approaches. Those were the three pieces of our mission. Now our mission has shifted. It's still about adults; it's still about degree completion; but 85% of the activity that our students engage in is taking online courses. We're still a transfer institution in the sense that you come in with credits, but then you do the rest of your work with us. I would say that's a shift in our identity.

What we are trying to do is be a major participant in the adult-degree marketplace, because it's good for the country and it's good for the economy, and it's what we were built to do. We believe that if you're going to educate adults, you have to have a scalable product, and online's the only way to do that.

We're flexible, affordable, and adult-focused. So if you're 25 or older and you haven't got a degree yet, you should look at us. What do you need to know? We can help you learn it. We have figured out a way to give you a structured learning experience, whether that's a test or portfolio or course or something else, that you can do from wherever you are.

President George Pruitt on Thomas Edison State College

Thomas Edison State College was founded in 1972. It was created as part of a movement that was stimulated by a series of Carnegie reports in the '60s that highlighted the special requirements and needs of older adult students. The adults first came into the academy following World War II, as a result of the GI Bill, and the assumption was that these students would come in and sort of be a bubble passing through the system and then go away. By the middle '60s, it was fairly clear that adults were continuing to come into the marketplace and into college in ways that you could not associate with the GI Bill, and that was actually creating challenges for colleges and universities, because the policy context for them was around the needs and requirements of 18-year-olds. So the colleges were trying to figure out what to do with these "nontraditional students." And at that time, they were post-traditional.

Well, what the Carnegie Commission suggested was that colleges and universities create a special policy focus on adults: that adults are not 18-year-olds who have just been around longer. They have special needs and requirements, and they bring special talents and assets to the community that traditional-aged students don't. They concluded you can't accommodate adults and traditional-aged students within the same framework.

As a result of that, several states responded: New York created the Regents External Degree Program and Empire State College; New Jersey created Thomas Edison State College; Connecticut created Charter Oak; Minnesota created Minnesota Metropolitan State College. What all of these institutions had in common was, "Thou shall serve adult students."

Thomas Edison was created to be a combination of Empire and Regents—we did pretty much the things that both of them did. Regents basically did a lot of credit evaluation, transfer credit, credit for prior learning. Empire had an independent study model. Thomas Edison sort of did both.

We were founded here in Trenton, but when the college was first formed, we were actually on Princeton University's campus. In 1979, we moved into a beautiful building in downtown Trenton, and we've been here ever since. We have made a commitment to the city and purposely moved into our state capital. We are the only public institution of higher education headquartered in our capital city. But we are not a place-dependent or time-dependent kind of school. We really could have been anywhere, and we chose to be in our capital city.

What's special about Thomas Edison (and about Excelsior) is that we were created to serve adults. Now, that's usually not how you start a college. Usually you start a college around what you're going to offer. Are you going to be a business school, or a research university, or a teacher's college, or a liberal arts college? Or you do it around a geography—a territory that you're going to serve. For us, it wasn't what you offer, and it wasn't where you offered it. The issue was the clients that you would serve. And the issue was: you will serve self-directed adult students. When you start a college around who the clients are going to be, and your clients are different, you end up being a very different institution.

The two principal characteristics of adult students are that the access barriers they face are the barriers of time and place. They can't put their careers, jobs, families on hold to go sit in a classroom somewhere on Monday, Wednesday, and Friday. The other characteristic they have is that learning is continuous, and many students, many adult students, have accumulated or achieved college-level capacities and competencies in non-collegiate environments.

Today we have over 18,000 students. We're the only public college in New Jersey that offers degrees at the associate, baccalaureate, and graduate levels. We have over 20 degree programs, over 100 majors spread over those 20 degree programs. We're a state college in New Jersey. Two-thirds of our students are from New Jersey, but the other third are from every state in America and 84 countries throughout the world.

We have a small, five-building campus in downtown Trenton, surrounding the state capital complex. We have about 300 full-time employees, and we have about another 600 to 700 scholars and mentors that we use on an as-needed basis and who come in and out— people who have scholarly training and capacity.

We don't describe ourselves as a distance-learning school. This is one of the things we fight against. The press and the public try to put a handle on us. It's certainly something we do, and it's one of our core competencies, but it is not who we are. We're more involved in prior learning assessment than most colleges in the country. That's another of our core competencies, but that's not who we are, either. We have a variety of ways that students can study independently with us and earn credit through examinations. So sometimes people call us an independent study school. Once again, it's one of the things we do, but it's not who we are. Those are all arrows in the quiver.

Our mission statement is in one sentence: Thomas Edison State College was created to provide flexible, high-quality, collegiate learning opportunities for self-directed adults. That is who we are. We don't have any traditional classroom instruction, so there are no students here taking classes. There are several ways that students earn credits for us. If you want a classroom experience, you can enroll at a traditional college, take the course to satisfy our degree requirement, and transfer it back. We have students enrolled in every public and private college in New Jersey, taking courses to satisfy our degree requirements.

The other extreme is you can study on your own and sit for an examination, or take an examination for things that you already know, or go through a portfolio assessment process. In the middle is every kind of technology-supported learning opportunity that is available anywhere in the world. The way our students earn credit is that they pick and choose from the various methodologies available to them until they have satisfied the graduation requirements.

We are unabashedly committed to being a special-purpose institution, and we circle the wagons around our mission of serving self-directed adults. In fact, you have to be at least 21 before you can even apply to Thomas Edison. We will not admit a student under the age of 21, unless they're in the military or unless they have an associate's degree from an accredited community college. The average age in our student body is about 40.

We operate year-round. We start a new term every month. You start whenever you want to start. You graduate whenever you finish. We have a commencement ceremony once a year in October for people who want a robe, and who want to go through the ceremony of celebrating the academic achievement.

We have two fee structures: one is sort of the à la carte version, and the other is the all-you-can-eat plan. The à la carte version depends on what you pick and choose from all these various methods that I have described. The all-you-can-eat plan for New Jersey students is around $4,600 a year. It's very affordable. It includes every-thing—all you can eat.

We're similar to Excelsior in that we started around the same time, with the same movement, and were part of the same body of research. There were a group of schools that kind of hung out together: Empire, Regents that later became Excelsior, Thomas Edison, University of Maryland University College, and there were a few others in the early days. The School of New Resources at the College of New Rochelle in New York was one. But there was a core group of adult-serving institutions. We grew up together; we have collaborated extensively over the years; we have shared processes and policies and advocacy of adult learners with each other. There are similarities we all have, and I think there are things that differ-entiate us. We all developed independently. What calibrated us was that we had the same clients, so we were forced to deal with the same problems and same kinds of people and we came up with variations of the same solution.

When you ask my students why they are here, I believe they will say that it's unfinished business—that they started their education at some earlier point, then life got in the way. However, they do understand the value of an education. Most of our students have jobs—correction, they don't have jobs, they have careers. We have a lot of senior citizens who have retired. They're here for their own fulfillment and to achieve what for them is a life objective—one that is important to them for a variety of reasons.

President Robert Mendenhall on Western Governors University

We were founded in 1997 by nineteen Western governors, from Hawaii to Indiana, to expand access and opportunity for education. The governors could see the day when the states couldn't just keep building more buildings and pouring more money into higher education, so it was really created for several reasons: as a private nonprofit that would offer additional opportunity in the states; in particular, as a school that would use technology to be more productive in the delivery of education; and to implement a new model in higher education that measured learning rather than time. We were set up to be a competency-based institution that would actually define what graduates should know and be able to do. When they're able to demonstrate that they can do it, they graduate.

So we are entirely online, but we are very different than other online institutions. Traditional online education, whether from the University of Phoenix or the University of Michigan, is basically a professor teaching a class. We just moved the classroom to the Internet, and we're using the technology to distribute the classroom, not to really change the model of education. In our case, we're using the computer to do the teaching, to deliver the content. Our faculty do not develop or teach courses. We define the competencies expected of a graduate. We develop the assessments to measure those competencies. And we then go find the learning resources that map to those competencies that teach them well, wherever they are.

There are now two million courses on the Internet. So there's no need for us to develop our own and claim they're the best. Instead, we have our faculty go find the best available courses, and we acquire the rights to use them with our students. The faculty then are full-time, and their full-time role is mentoring students through the program—guiding, directing, answering questions, modeling, motivating, encouraging, supporting. Most other fully online universities are for-profit, and they're basically using adjunct faculty. And, frankly, most of our traditional universities are using a lot of adjunct faculty for teaching online courses, as well. At WGU, we essentially have full-time faculty who mentor students.

We have students in all 50 states. We have mentors in 40 states. We actually have two different types, or levels, of mentoring. So when a student starts at WGU, they get a mentor who stays with them from the beginning of their program until they complete it— until the very end. And that's in very much of an advisor and mentor role. Then, as they go into each content area—each course, if you will—there's a mentor for that course material who is an expert in that particular content area and mentors them through that area. So they have one mentor who stays with them from beginning to end, and then as they move from subject to subject, they have other mentors who support the subjects.

Our students are certainly turned loose to learn at their own pace, to demonstrate what they know, to spend their time on what they don't know, and to learn those new things at a pace they can determine. The mentor is really there to guide them to the right resources and to help them understand what they know and don't know. Almost all of our mentors work out of their homes with a telephone and a computer. They never actually meet physically with the students. It's all delivered online, and they're guiding them through the programs. The protocol is every week, or every other week, conversations on the phone.

We're right around 20,000 students, across all 50 states. We're still growing about 35% a year. We had 14,000 students this time last year, so we're still growing very rapidly. The average age of a WGU student is 36, but they range from 16 to 76; a pretty normal bell curve around 36. About 70% of them work full-time while they're going to school, and 75% of them are underserved—either low-income, first generation in their family to attend college, minority, or rural student who wouldn't otherwise have access. So we're generally addressing working adults, and WGU provides a unique opportunity for them to gain a degree and move into a better career.

We just do bachelor's and master's degrees; we don't do associate's degrees, and we don't do doctorates. We do degrees in four areas: business, information technology, teacher education, and healthcare, including nursing. Why those areas? Because those are big workforce needs in the country, and we're set up to help adults get an education and move into the workforce and be successful. We're also one of the five largest teachers colleges in the country: we've got between 8,000 and 9,000 students in our teachers college. We're probably the largest provider of math and science teachers in the country. We've got about 2,000 enrolled in math and science teaching.

People ask all the time how we do all of this online. Yes, we're online, but our teachers do student teaching in a classroom, with a host teacher and a clinical supervisor, and they're evaluated on eight separate rubrics that we've developed that demonstrate their competency. We're the only online university that's accredited by NCATE, which is the teacher accreditation, and the only teachers college in the country that can license our graduates in all 50 states.

We have six-month terms. We start new students every month, so you can sign up the first of every month and you go for a six-month term. The terms run consecutively. It's $2,890 per term, so basically $5,800 for a 12-month year. That covers all of our costs, so we're self-sustaining on tuition of $5,800 a year, and because we free students up to not spend time on what they already know, and let them learn at their own pace what they don't know, our average time to graduation with a bachelor's degree is 29 months.

We don't have credit hours or grades. We just have competencies, and when you can demonstrate the competencies, you graduate. It's a really simple premise. We know that people come to higher education already knowing different things and having different skills, and we know that people learn at different rates. Yet we have a higher education system that says, "Everybody needs 120 credit hours; everybody needs the same required courses; and every course takes four months." So by definition, it's highly inefficient. That's not the way we learn. It assumes that everybody comes as a blank slate and everybody learns at the same rate. We simply blew that up and said, "Come to WGU, demonstrate the competencies you have, spend time on the competencies you don't have, spend as much time as you need to master them, and when you've mastered them, demonstrate it and move on. So it's productive for the student.

We're the only university actually granting degrees based solely on demonstrated competency. But where we hope we fit is as a demonstration of a new way of doing education that actually uses technology not just to distribute classroom education but to change the way we deliver education—namely, to make it individualized and self-paced. And to demonstrate that you can actually measure learning as opposed to just measuring time. And ultimately to show that it can be very high-quality and very affordable. I mentioned tuition is $5,800 a year—we haven't raised tuition in the last four years, and don't plan to raise it in the next couple of years. The goal is to grow our own productivity fast enough that we can give our people raises every year and not raise tuition. So far we've been able to do that.

I'm impressed with the governors who wrote the original mission: to expand access and to improve the quality of higher education by providing this education independent of time and place, and establishing competency-based criteria for graduation. I think we're the model of the future in two ways: one, we're going to have to use technology to be more productive; and two, we're going to have to start measuring learning rather than time. We want to expand access, especially to students who are typically shut out; we want to improve quality; we want to make it more affordable; and we want to be responsive to workforce needs and to develop degree programs accepted by employers. We've been trying to do that for the last 13 years, and we're still at it.

President Alan Davis on Empire State College

We were founded in 1971. Along with Excelsior, we're celebrating our 40th anniversary. Our mission is pretty straightforward. We focus on breaking down the barriers that normally interfere with people accessing higher education—issues of time, place, pace, previous experience with education—and we try to focus on providing rigorous education to people, of any age, who are motivated to study with us. We also try to honor their informal or formal learning that they have gained previously, through college or work experience.

Our pedagogical model is based on the mentor/learner interface. That is, every learner is assigned a faculty mentor. The students then work with those mentors to design their own programs of study that will fit their particular needs, that embrace the learning that came before, and that will bridge them to the goals that they want to achieve. There is a process of exploration and educational planning which leads to a degree plan that then is approved by the faculty and the college in order for the student to move ahead.

This model of individualized study and individualized degree plans, which I like to call personalized, is the core of our learning experience. Some of the people I read, who talk about the future of digital technologies and the impact on education, very quickly come to the conclusion that with every student able to connect to everything and everyone in more and more sophisticated ways, it's really going to move to a personalized learning model. Because students are going to be able to go and access resources from all kinds of places, they're going to want to study what they want, when they want, and how they want, simply because they can, and then if they want their learning credentialed, they can come to someplace like Empire State or Excelsior.

But it's going to be very personalized. The personal computer leads to personalized learning, which leads to personalized programs, and we already have that, of course. The evolution of the digital world has brought us to this convergence with our individualized model, and that's where I think our model of learning is better. We don't have to unpack the classrooms, the traditions, the lectures, the curriculums, or the sequential courses.

We have very flexible delivery options, both online and on-site, so the students we look for are really those for whom the traditional system does not work. We do require two things: a high school diploma or the equivalent, and we ask people to submit, in writing, a rationale for why they want to study with us. It's an essay question, and we then mark the essay according to a rubric, and we admit those who we think are ready, or close to being ready, for college-level study. Clearly, if someone isn't writing in a manner that we can recognize as something that's going to get them started, we don't admit them. We don't offer formal courses in remediation for these people, but we do have a program that we can refer people to if they're not ready.

We offer a very open curriculum, with eleven areas of study at the undergraduate level. We have broad guidelines for those areas of study, plus the SUNY general education requirements. Within those fairly loose guidelines, the students can build any program they like, and they can get a BA or a BS in areas such as Business Management and Economics, in Community and Human Services, in Science, Math and Technology, and in a number of others. That's their major, in a sense, and then they can develop a concentration in almost any area that makes sense. We also have a small undergraduate nursing program that started two years ago. We offer four-year degrees and master's programs, with an MA in Teaching, an MBA, and several other graduate degrees.

Empire State currently enrolls 20,200 students, with an average age of 36. We serve students from every county in New York State. Our coordinating center is in Saratoga Springs. Sometimes people show up here and they look on the SUNY map and they see Empire State College in Saratoga Springs, and they think, *Well, that looks nice*, and they say, "Let's send our kid there." We have to explain to them, "Well, we don't really have a campus here. We have some offices here, but we don't actually have a campus." Once they understand that, it's better. What we do have are 35 physical locations around the state, and probably close to a dozen internationally, where we actually operate on-site, one way or another.

We also have about 60,000 alumni now, and we're ranked #1 in student satisfaction among the SUNY colleges and universities. We're proud of that, but that's not unusual for adult-focused institutions. Adults tend to be more generous. They come to us by choice, and we try to treat them very well. And although I tend to become frustrated by all the regulations and guidelines inherent in being part of a large public system of education, one main advantage is that Empire State does award a SUNY degree. That has a lot of currency, and it's very helpful for students.

We are actually an open institution. Excelsior is an open institution. Thomas Edison and Charter Oak and Western Governors are our peers. We are, by my definition, the institutions that have been given a special mandate to reach out to those not being served by traditional higher education. We separate ourselves from traditional institutions, who are selective, and who are closed in the sense of, "You have to be here; you have to sit in front of me, you have to study what I say." We and our sister institutions just take a whole different approach. Everybody who comes and wants to study, we take. As long as they've got a high school diploma, and they can read and write to a level that we can see is going to get them started, we take them.

Education for a New Age

George Keller, in *Higher Education and the New Society*, writes: ". . . the nation's colleges and universities urgently need to break out of their century-old structures and redesign the delivery of advanced education and training for the new age."

The Council for Adult and Experiential Learning (CAEL) has recently released a study of 62,475 student records at 48 colleges and universities. Among the findings:

- Students with credits obtained through prior learning assessment (PLA) had higher graduation rates. More than 56% of PLA students earned a postsecondary degree within seven years, while only 21% of those without did so.
- Students with PLA credit showed greater persistence. Even those students who had not earned a degree by year seven showed greater amounts of credit accumulation than those without PLA credit. More than half of those who had yet to earn a degree by 2008 (end of the study period) had accumulated 80% or more of needed credits by that point. This compares with 22% of non-PLA students with no degree who had reached this level of progress.
- Students with PLA credit need less time to graduate. PLA students earning bachelor's degrees saved on average of between 2.5 and 10.1 months of time in earning their degrees.

Institutions seeking to respond to President Obama's challenge, and to consider the country's needs, may wish to consider open enrollment at least for adult programs, the assessment of prior learning, credit-by-exam, and more liberal transfer policies. The non-profit institutions we have discussed here have embraced many, if not all, of these practices. Together, they seek to assist those who have not always been well served by traditional higher education — including the many adults with some credit but no degree.

– 7 –

Elizabeth Bewley:
Seeking a Broader Canvas

After years in the workforce, Elizabeth Bewley earned her BA from Excelsior, went on to attain her MBA from Columbia University, enjoyed a successful career as an executive with Johnson & Johnson, and is now an author who has written an important new book about health-care in America. Her accomplishments illustrate what happens when capable and talented people discover a path that finally works for them.

My life has been saved on at least three occasions by doctors and hospitals. The first time was when I was 15. I had some kind of an allergic reaction. They weren't sure to what, but I almost stopped breathing. My mother took me to the doctor's office, and just in the time that I was waiting to see the doctor, my breathing got dramatically worse. He stopped in the doorway, shocked, and looked at me, and then he told the nurse to call the hospital and set up an emergency admission.

When I got to the hospital, I was having tremendous difficulty breathing. They set me up in a bed and told me that if I needed anything, I should press the call button. Now, my doctor had me confined to bed. I wasn't allowed to get up and use the bathroom or anything. And I couldn't talk because of all the swelling. They didn't have me on a breathing machine, and nobody was in the room, monitoring me.

Of course, this was a number of years ago, and they didn't have the kind of monitoring equipment that is common today. They set up this blue package on the nightstand, next to the bed, and I asked what it was. It was this big bulky thing, and they said it was a tracheotomy tray. I was doing all this in writing because I couldn't talk. My mother had brought me there, but she had to go back to work. She was director of the public library in Haddonfield, New Jersey. So they told me, "If your breathing gets any worse, we're going to have to slice your throat open and put a breathing tube in there. The reason we would do it here is that you would be dead by the time we could get you to an operating room, which is three floors away."

I'm sure that my heart rate went up some. I was lying there; I couldn't talk; I couldn't move; I couldn't get out of bed. And my doctor had also told me not to try to whisper, because he felt that if I tried to whisper that it would irritate my throat further and that might close my throat completely. The allergic reaction was clearly the problem—my throat was almost swollen shut. But at the time, no one even knew it was an allergic reaction. They were coming up with diagnoses like acute endotracheal bronchitis. That's technical speak for everything-in-your-throat-swells-up.

So I was lying there, and after I had been there for a few hours, I pressed the call button. Now, they had told me, because of the situation, "You're going to be pressing the call button for lots of things. But whenever you press the call button, someone is going to come running, because they're not going to know if it's an emergency or not, and you can't tell them because you can't talk. But they're going to be prepared. If you press the call button because your breathing has gotten worse, they've got about three minutes to get you breathing again."

Well, they were trying to impress me that I didn't need to be worried. Whenever I pressed the call button, somebody would come running. They were trying to un-terrify me. I mean, it was a scary situation. So, a few hours in, my mother was gone, and I pressed the call button. This little voice came over the intercom and said, "What do you need?" Well, I couldn't talk, and I wasn't going to try to whisper, since my doctor had impressed upon me that it was important not to.

I didn't answer, and I thought, *If I don't answer, they'll send somebody*. But that's not what happened. A moment later, the voice said, "If you don't say what you need, no one will come." To this day, I have flashbacks about that moment. I have this indelible image of that speaker grille on the wall, about five feet away from where I was, because that was the face of healthcare—the speaker grille for the intercom. I'm sure if somebody had been in the room, they would have seen me freeze. I just instantly had the realization that I could die right then, in the hospital, with the surgical means to save my life less than two feet away.

I was terrified, and in fact, no one came for about twenty minutes—the longest twenty minutes of my life. And then a nurse came tearing into the room, skidding across the floor as she came in. She was breathing hard, and she had her hand to her chest, and she was trying to catch her breath, and she saw that I was okay. She apologized profusely, and she told me it would never happen again, and it didn't for the five days I was in the hospital. But all it would have taken was once.

That was the first hint I had that the promise of healthcare to save lives can fall apart. You think about everything available, and there are tremendous amounts of resources that are available: drugs, and medical devices, and well-trained, well-intentioned doctors and nurses, hospitals, and all sorts of things. They can save lives, and they do. I made it out of the hospital alive, and it was questionable when I went in. It was tricky. They do save lives.

But there's another side to healthcare. There's a lot of flawed thinking that goes on, and it puts patients at risk, and it kills hundreds of thousands of people every year. Fifteen million people:

that's the number of people who are injured in a hospital every year. That's the number from reputable studies that have been done. And the problem is not one of technology, but of attitude.

In that situation with me, you might think that what would go on in the mind of somebody on the other end of that intercom might be, *Gee, this is a hospital, and the children here are pretty sick. If someone presses a call button and doesn't say anything, maybe I better send somebody to find out what's wrong.* That would be a reasonable response. But what seems to have gone on was more like, *If a child presses a call button and then doesn't say anything, they must be fooling around. I had a five-year-old boy here two weeks ago and he just got a kick out of pressing the call button. That's probably what's going on here. This kid is probably just pressing the call button and fooling around, too, and I'm not going to stand for that. I don't have time for that. I'll show her who's in charge.* It could easily have been something like that, right?

Okay, now, wait a minute. That stereotypes the patient as being the worst example of the patients that a nurse or doctor sees. But I was a 15-year-old, incredibly well-behaved, and a terrified kid, and this was the first time I had pressed the call button during the three hours I had been there. I was confined to bed, so maybe I would have needed to use the bathroom or something, right? So whoever heard that call button had an agenda of her own, and the agenda there was about control. It was about who gets to call the shots. *I'm not letting some kid tell me what to do. They have to conform to my requirements. I'm in charge.*

This is just one example of a kind of attitude in healthcare that can lead directly to patients' deaths. In my case, it didn't, of course, but it could have, and do you know what the death certificate would have said? It would say that she died of endotracheal bronchitis, or respiratory arrest, or something like that. It wouldn't say that a bad attitude in the healthcare system killed this patient. And there are dozens, hundreds, thousands of similar ways in which attitudes about patients interfere with them getting the care they need, or even some of the technology that might save them. This isn't about money. It isn't about anything but treating patients with respect.

I don't normally blow my own horn, but I will tell you that in the book that I've just written, *Killer Cure*, I go through many, many similar stories to build my case — to explain how many people actually die and are injured from healthcare. The book has nearly 500 endnotes in it, because I have been very careful to document every fact I provide. I use that first hospital story of mine to illustrate how I personally understand the danger as well. Toward the end of the book, I talk about what the real underlying problem is, and the analogy I use is that patients today are in a very similar situation to slaves before emancipation or to women before they got the right to vote. They're treated as people who don't have the intelligence, competence, interest, or mental wherewithal to be able to make decisions about their own care. Their needs and their priorities are tremendously discounted, and they end up dying or being injured for no good reason.

What I want to emphasize here, though, is that I could never have written this book if I had not worked as an executive at Johnson & Johnson for almost 20 years, and I wouldn't have gotten that great job if I had not earned my MBA from Columbia University and interned with J&J in the summer between my two years at grad school. And none of it would have happened if I had never heard of Excelsior College.

I grew up in New Jersey and graduated from Haddonfield Memorial High School.

When I was 18, I went to Grinnell College in Grinnell, Iowa, and spent a couple of years there. Then I felt like I needed to do something else. It just wasn't a good fit at the time to continue in college. I had been waiting from the age of 7 to go to college. I had been marking time, because I had been raised to believe that college was the answer to everything. College would solve all your problems; college would open doors to all kinds of opportunities; college would make clear what my life was to be about. So I went to college with expectations that probably no college could have met, and I became disillusioned, but it wasn't the fault of any particular school.

I was at Grinnell, in Iowa, from 1971 until 1973, and I studied a variety of things that I had never been exposed to before—sociology, psychology, theater. But after about two years at Grinnell, I didn't feel that I was any closer to understanding what I was doing with my life. And I was tremendously idealistic. I left school and did a variety of non-profit things. It was the '70s, so there were some New Age things, but my goal in whatever I did was to try to figure out how to make the world a better place. Whatever I did during that time, I was trying to be a constructive person. But where I ended up was doing bookkeeping and accounting for a number of different, small organizations. I felt like what I was doing wasn't making much of a difference, and that I didn't really have much of a future. At that point I decided to go back to school.

One of the things that I wanted, and I don't think it was unusual, was that I felt a degree would ensure that I had a way to support myself for the rest of my life. I decided I would get a degree in accounting, and I would sit for the CPA exam. Then, at least, I would always have that in my back pocket. I was confident that I would always be able to get a job with that. I started looking at all the ways I could return to school, and it seemed to me that there were a lot of obstacles.

For example, in that little organization where I was working at the time, my boss kept talking about opening another office in another city, and he thought he might send me there to run that. During tax season, I would be working 80 or 90 hours a week, and I definitely wouldn't be able to take classes. I did end up taking a few classes, and it seemed enormously time-consuming. I realized that if I could take one or maybe two classes a semester, it would take me about five years to complete the number of credits I would need to get an accounting degree, because not everything in the two years I had completed at Grinnell was going to count for the business requirements.

It seemed daunting to have to spend every waking minute of my life for the next five years trying to complete that degree, and then thinking it probably wasn't going to work anyway. My boss might end up transferring me, or I'd have to drop out during tax season. It all just seemed unworkable. I went looking for other approaches. I found a book by John Bear that talked about different ways to complete a degree, and Excelsior College (Regents at the time) was mentioned.

I looked at that and thought, *You know, I think I can do this.* To make a long story short, I completed about two and a half years of requirements in 16 months while working full-time during tax season, sitting at my kitchen table and doing nothing else. I was living on things like canned soup so I wouldn't have to go to the grocery store too often, and the only break I had was in the evening when I would take a walk for about half an hour.

I had started out thinking, *Really, I know all of this accounting stuff. I just have to get the degree to prove it—to have the credential.* Well, it turned out that what I knew about accounting and finance covered maybe the first semester of one course. I actually learned an enormous amount while completing the degree, and it changed my entire idea of what I wanted to do with my life—in particular, the work on business strategy. There was a capstone course at the time in business policy and strategy, and it really made an impression on me.

In 16 months, I completed two and a half years of credits and I graduated with an accounting degree on the CPA track. But in the course of doing that, everything changed: I realized that I didn't want to be an accountant anymore. I had become far more interested in the other things I was learning. There were all these things I hadn't known existed. So I had the degree in accounting, but it was no longer what I wanted to do. At that point, I decided, *Oh, I'm going to have to go to graduate school. I'm going to have to go and get an MBA to do the kind of work that I'm interested in doing.*

I had a great belief in the potential for organizations to be a positive force in society. I had been knocking around in the non-profit and small business world for decades, and I was interested in going in a different direction and seeing what large organizations could do. I decided I was going to graduate school, and fortunately I knew almost nothing about MBA programs. If I had, I would have realized that the odds were stacked against me, as somebody who had dropped out of college and gotten a degree in an unusual way. In other words, I had not spent the intervening time on Wall Street. Again, out of complete ignorance, I decided that if I was going to go to graduate school, what I needed to do was go to one of the Top Ten, so that there would be no question about my ability at that level. So I applied to Columbia University.

Well, I got a call from Columbia, saying they were reviewing my application and that I needed to show up in person for an interview. Now that raised some red flags, because in their admissions materials they said they almost never interviewed people. They typically worked on the materials that people sent in. Okay. I was in Florida at the time, so I made the arrangements to go to New York for the interview. I packed my briefcase with materials to prove the legitimacy of the Regents External Degree and Exam Program— accreditation materials and everything. Well, when I got there and started the interview, they said, "Oh, we know that. That's not an issue. We've admitted other people from there. That's not the question. The question is, you know, you dropped out of college and you've been doing this small business and non-profit stuff. You just don't look like corporate material."

The whole Regents/Excelsior thing was not an issue for Columbia. I did not have a problem getting into Columbia because of my Regents degree. I had a problem getting into Columbia because I had dropped out of college. But I had written in my admissions essay about "Live Aid," the concert, and talked about how it struck me that the organizer of that was about my age, early 30s, and he was making a significant impact with something. That was what I wanted to do as well: I wanted to have a positive impact on the world, on a large scale, and I guess I was just compelling enough in the interview that they accepted me.

I went to graduate school at Columbia from 1986 until 1988. I went on to chair the Student Faculty Academic Affairs Committee. I was on the Honor Roll, I believe, every semester. I was inducted into Beta Gamma Sigma, the honor society for business school. I won a competitive scholarship for leadership. I won an award voted on by students for someone who had made a big impact on the school. So I did very well there—until the last semester, and this brings us back to healthcare.

I came down with an ear infection and I went to the student health clinic. I was diagnosed with a middle ear infection, and I was treated for five months or so, and the doctor was getting increasingly frustrated with me because I wasn't getting better. So he decided to slice my eardrum open to drain the fluid that was in my middle ear.

And then he told me my problems were over: "I solved the problem; I got the fluid out."

That night, I didn't sleep very well, because about every half hour I was awakened by another wet spot on my pillow. The cotton ball in my ear had gotten completely saturated and had overflowed onto the pillow, and the wet pillow kept waking me. So I would take out the cotton ball and throw it on the mat by the bed, and then insert a dry one. When I woke up in the morning, there were 13 wet cotton balls on the mat.

Later that morning I was talking to my sister about it, and she said, "Something is really wrong. You have to call the doctor and talk to him about it." And I said, "It's Saturday, and I won't get him anyway, because he's only at the student health clinic for two hours on Wednesday." I was really crying, and she said, "No, something's really wrong. You have to call him somehow."

"I'm really tired and I'm not going to be able to get him anyway," I repeated. "I'm just not going to do it."

On Monday, fluid stopped coming out, and I saw the doctor for a post-op check-up the following Wednesday. And I started to tell him about the 13 cotton balls and all the fluid, and he just snapped. He said, "That's ridiculous. That didn't happen." And I was so taken aback that I just didn't say anything else. I was 34 or so at the time, and I was very well respected. Nobody accused me of lying about anything. And here was this guy who was essentially calling me a liar.

So, okay, he tells me again I'm cured — post-op check-up, we're done. A week later, Wednesday afternoon, I was back in his office, and he concludes once again that there was fluid in my ear, and he was really, really angry with me. He looked at me and he said, "How did this happen?"

I saw him a couple of days after that, and he finds fluid in my ear again, and this time he decides he'll put a tube in my ear. He won't just slice the eardrum open and let it drain; he'll put a tube in there. And I was appalled by this, and by the idea that I would have fluid constantly dripping out of my head.

He scheduled the operation for the very end of the school year, a couple of days before graduation, and he sliced my eardrum open again and suctioned out all the fluid with a little vacuum cleaner and he tried to put the tube in but he couldn't get it to stay in. So he stepped away and was preparing more material to try it again, and then he stopped. He just dead stopped, and he said, "There's more fluid in your ear." And I was looking at him, like, *Yeah, why is this a surprise to you?*

Then he got frantic, very fast, and this plan was put in place: I would be admitted to the hospital for brain surgery shortly after graduation. Turned out, at the end of the day, there was no roof to my middle ear, and apparently that was congenital, and there was a pinprick hole in the dural membrane surrounding the brain right above the ear. Nobody knows why that appeared, although I have my theories related to some of the treatments that he did, that I think caused some trouble. So I had cerebral spinal fluid dripping straight from my brain into my ear.

The concept of putting a tube in was crazy: that would have opened a direct channel from the outside air directly into my brain, and I'm lucky that I didn't get meningitis and die after the first time that he sliced my eardrum open. That would have caused a big, open hole to the outside ear. And I wasn't particularly paying attention to dramatically sterile processes when I was shoving cotton balls in there, either. So I was just really lucky that I didn't die in that intervening time.

In one realm of my life, I'm winning awards in Columbia University's graduate business school, and in another realm, I'm being treated by a doctor as if I couldn't possibly have a single accurate thing to say, as if I was completely mistaken about my own body or, worst case scenario, that I was just lying about everything and that I had fabricated all the fluid coming out. In my regular day-to-day life, I was a well-regarded professional, but as soon as I walked into that doctor's office, I might as well have been two years old and have been completely incapable of voicing an articulate thought. That's exactly what I meant with my analogy about slaves and about women who didn't have the right to vote. It's completely disenfranchising.

There were challenges, but I made it through. I had interned in the summer between the two years of graduate school at Johnson & Johnson, and before I left at the end of the summer, they made me an offer for full-time employment—to come back after I graduated. I interviewed with a lot of companies, and I decided that Johnson & Johnson was the best. It was the end of 1987, beginning of 1988 and, as you might recall, the second of the two Tylenol tamperings had happened, I think, in 1986. Some crazy person, not related to Johnson & Johnson, was trying to get back at a family member or something, and they inserted toxins into the bottles.

I was very, very impressed with how Johnson & Johnson had behaved. I didn't want to throw my weight behind any organization that wasn't going to behave ethically. So with the whole Tylenol thing fresh in my mind, I thought, *This is a company that really does put its money where its mouth is. It's serious about putting the patient first, about putting the customer first, because it just spent hundreds of millions of dollars to try to address an issue that it didn't cause in the first place.* I went to work for them.

Well, I stayed with J&J for 20 years, and for most of that time I was an executive. I was hired in through an MBA hiring program, with the idea that after three years, I would either make it to manager or we would probably come to some amicable parting. Ten months after I started, I was a manager. And then about a year or so after that, I was promoted to the director level, though I didn't have a director title. But I had eight managers reporting to me. In about two years, I had gotten to a level which generally took people about 15 years to get to. I was the first woman to be promoted to that level.

By 1990, I was in operations, renamed Product Supply, and ironically I was in charge of making sure that Wal-Mart had Tylenol on its shelves. I had probably a $30 million budget for what I was doing. I went from operations roles, at the request of the number-two man at J&J, to being in charge of the $200 million Information Technology Project, about which I knew nothing. I kept telling him that, and he kept saying, "I want somebody who has been successful at running things, and you have."

I did that for four years, but I had decided that I also needed to formally study the healthcare system in America. I thought, *If I'm going to be in this, I need to understand it.* At that point, I had gone through two life-changing experiences with the healthcare system. I was working in it, and I had the feeling that I really didn't get it. I decided to study it.

I found a program through City University in Bellevue, Washington, their graduate program in Health Policy, which I completed several courses in. I did not go for the degree there, because it would have duplicated much of my MBA from Columbia. And they would not transfer credits, which I thought was interesting. I took the courses that were relevant to me, and got an enormous amount out of that.

In 1996, I really developed a strong sense that patients were the underdogs. There were 300 million of them, more or less, in this country, but they were still the underdogs. And I also realized that things needed to be very, very different. So from that point on, I started paying a lot of attention every day to news reports and so forth. When the Internet became a viable resource and I started getting electronic news clipping services, I began to accumulate an enormous amount of information and research studies that painted a pretty sad picture.

It became so clear to me that what really needed to happen to get healthcare to work in America was that the patient (although I really shouldn't call them patients, because that puts them one-down in relation to doctors)—that people really need to be at the center of the equation in healthcare. That's why I say that healthcare needs to define its purpose as enabling people to lead the lives they want. It shouldn't be to improve population health or anything else. It should be to help people lead the lives they want.

I started to develop this realization that patients were being mistreated, not because anybody had bad intentions, but for a whole host of historical reasons. In 2004, I began to make the case inside Johnson & Johnson that I should focus on what is required to get healthcare to work better in this country. I will forever be grateful to J&J that they allowed me to stay and to get focused on that, and that really became a focus on putting people at the center of the equation.

Finally, I reached a point when I had done as much as I could from inside the company. I thought I had to write a book to put together what I had learned. I didn't even ask, because I knew what the answer would have been. J&J execs don't go publishing books that can be interpreted as being critical of the healthcare industry, which comprises its major customers. This is not any kind of criticism of Johnson & Johnson. What I needed to do was healthcare system-wide. I felt that I needed a broader canvas, so to speak. So I left J&J in 2008 after 20 years there and, with my husband, relocated to Prescott, Arizona.

Everything that I've done has sort of contributed to getting to the point where I am, and the idea really is to make significant, positive change in the world—to make the world a better place. I chose as my focus to try to change healthcare and to help people understand how to deal with it. If I hadn't gotten what turned out to be an excellent education at Excelsior, I wouldn't have understood that I wanted to do something different with my life, and I may never have written my book. My experience at Excelsior absolutely provided the genesis for the rest of my career.

–8–

What Is Your Degree Worth?

Let's look at the numbers. Before deciding to go back to school and investing the money required, people may want some idea of what they might expect in return—the ROI, or "return on investment," that investors require. The College Board's latest report, "Education Pays 2010: The Benefits of Higher Education for Individuals and Society," makes it clear that students who pursue higher education and attain postsecondary degrees gain financial and personal benefits: "The evidence is overwhelming that higher education improves people's lives, makes our economy more efficient, and contributes to a more equitable society . . . taxpayers and society as a whole derive a multitude of direct and indirect benefits when citizens have access to postsecondary education."

Consider the following statistics from that report:

- Median earnings of bachelor's degree recipients working full-time year-round in 2008 were $55,700, $21,900 more than median earnings of high school graduates.
- Individuals with some college but no degree earned 17% more than high school graduates working full-time year-round.

- For young adults between the ages of 20 and 24, the unemployment rate in the fourth quarter of 2009 for high school graduates was 2.6 times higher than for college graduates.
- In 2008, median earnings for women ages 25 to 34 with a bachelor's degree or higher were 79% greater than for those with a high school diploma. The earnings premium for men was 74%. A decade earlier, these earnings differentials were 60% and 54% respectively.
- The median hourly wage gain attributable to the first year of college, adjusted for race, gender, and work experience, increased from an estimated 8% in 1973 to about 10% in 1989 and 11% in 2007.
- In 2008, 8% of high school graduates ages 25 and older lived in households that relied on the Food Stamp Program, compared to just over 1% of those with at least a bachelor's degree. The pattern was similar for the National School Lunch Program.
- Spending on social support programs and incarceration costs are much lower for college graduates than for high school graduates. Estimated lifetime savings range from $32,600 for white women to $108,700 for black men. The gains in tax revenues produced by a more educated population are even greater.

The following list from the 2010 College Board report graphically illustrates the progressive differences in income:

Median Earnings for Full-time, Year-round Workers 25 and Older

Not a high school graduate	$24,300
High school graduate	33,800
Some college, no degree	39,700
Associate's degree	42,000
Bachelor's degree	55,700
Master's degree	67,300

Doctoral degree	91,900
Professional degree	100,000

The report also reveals that college-educated adults are more likely to receive health insurance and pension benefits from their employers, be satisfied with their jobs, have healthier lifestyles, engage in more educational activities with their children, and be more active as citizens than those who have not finished college.

In addition to greater personal income, a typical degree holder can also expect more stable employment. According to recent data from the Bureau of Labor Statistics, those without a high school diploma are unemployed at a rate of approximately 15%. Those with a high school diploma and some college, but no degree, are hovering at just under 10%, and those with a bachelor's degree are unemployed at a rate of less than 5%. Of course, having a degree does not guarantee that one will never be laid-off or fired. However, the re-employment options for those with a degree are significantly greater than for those without, all other factors being equal.

Even in good economic times with strong employment, those with academic credentials enjoy a hiring preference. A bachelor's degree signifies many things to an employer who is considering hiring or promoting you. It means you have completed 120 credit hours or more of learning and assessment. You have demonstrated an understanding of disparate subject matter, engaged in problem solving and critical thinking, and expressed yourself orally and in writing. While no degree guarantees mastery of a particular subject or field of study, it does demonstrate that you have satisfied minimum standards of learning and have developed the ability to produce acceptable levels of academic work and to meet deadlines set by others.

In the past few years, several critics of higher education have suggested that the cost of obtaining a degree is approaching a point where it exceeds the value that you can expect to receive in return. We maintain that this is not the case. There is no doubt that the cost of a degree, of whatever type, has been steadily increasing, although it is important to look more closely at what is actually happening.

The headlines decrying annual costs of $40,000 to $60,000 for tuition, room, board, and fees almost always refer to Ivy League or other highly selective institutions which understand that many people associate high price with better quality and greater prestige. Less well understood is that this is not only a conscious strategy on the part of these institutions, but that almost no one actually pays that amount. Nearly all private institutions engage in "discounting" as a way of attracting the type of student for which they want to be known. This practice, also known as "institutional support," can provide scholarships for athletes and applicants with stellar GPAs. Of course, these discounting plans seldom apply to adult students.

The other force exerting an impact on cost is the transfer of support for public institutions from taxpayers to the students who, presumably, will benefit from the instruction offered. Most public institutions now receive only a small percentage of their support from state government, and this is decreasing in the face of the current recession, forcing a rise in tuition and fees paid by students.

In order to pay for these increases, students have increasingly had to look for federal financial aid—Pell grants and Stafford loans—as well as other types of student loans. Some students have been profiled in the press as having assumed massive amounts of debt to earn degrees of questionable value. PBS broadcast a *Frontline* special in May 2010 titled "College, Inc." that accurately depicted the situation. However, it's also important to acknowledge that government policies are a primary reason for the increasing costs of higher education, and that the weak economy has severely affected access to employment and the ability of students to repay their education loans.

It comes then as no surprise that many students not only struggle to meet these rising costs but also leave college with substantial debt. The Project on Student Debt announced in its annual report that the average American college senior who graduated in

2009 owed $24,000 in student loans. In September 2010, US Secretary of Education Arne Duncan revealed that the student loan default rate for borrowers whose first loan repayments came due between October 2007 and September 2008, the last year for which figures were available, had climbed to 7%. Percentage rates of defaults rose across the board: 4% at private schools; 6% at public institutions; and 11.6% at for-profit universities. For the period of the study, 3.4 million borrowers entered repayment and 238,000 defaulted on their loans. More disturbing is the fact that, for the first time, people owe more for private and federal student loans than they do on their credit cards—$830 billion for education loans and $827 billion for credit card debt—and that more students are defaulting on those loans. In addition, The Institute for Higher Education Policy issued a report in March 2011 revealing that for every student who defaults, at least two more fall behind on their loan payments within the first five years after graduation.

This may sound obvious, but one of the best ways to avoid excessive student debt and to ensure a return on your educational investment is to be a smart consumer. There is no reason why anyone should have to pay even $100,000 ($25,000 a year) for a four-year undergraduate degree. People should be aware that going to an elite private school, where the number of applications actually increase with each year's rise in tuition, does not ensure success nor guarantee a great education.

Most associate's degrees require 60 semester units of credit. Community colleges are the primary source for this degree, and they're an incredible bargain: tuition rarely exceeds a few hundred dollars per credit at these schools, so your two-year degree should cost you between $6,000 and $18,000 ($100 to $300 per credit), plus fees and books.

At the bachelor's level, the usual requirement is 120 semester units. If the first 60 are from a community college, the remaining 60 can be earned at a private or public institution willing to accept your earlier work in transfer. However, be sure that your targeted four-year school will accept your community college credits, also known as "lower division" work, before following this path. While tuition at the "upper division" will likely cost more, there are a number of ways the overall cost can be reduced, especially for an adult student with prior experience. Electives within a degree program can often be fulfilled through "prior learning assessment." The American Council of Education (ACE) has reviewed thousands of military and corporate training programs and evaluated them for academic credit equivalency. The majority of regionally accredited institutions, public and private, accept these credit recommendations toward some categories of degree requirements.

Another form of prior learning assessment is credit-by-examination. With this process, students demonstrate their mastery of specified subject matter by taking a computer-delivered exam. The College Board, the Educational Testing Service, and Excelsior College are the primary sources. Costing little more than $100 per exam, they are an extremely inexpensive way to earn three to five units of credit. Excelsior College also offers a practice exam to help students measure their readiness for the official one. Excelsior is the only provider of this service to offer results on an academic transcript, which enhances the likelihood of acceptance by other institutions.

As previously noted, typical adult students bring transcripts from many other institutions with them. This work is evaluated and compared against a variety of degree requirements as part of the work to create a degree-completion plan for each student. Following this aggregation and assessment process, students understand what additional work will be required to earn their degrees. Typically, a student will need something less than 60 units of additional credit. These units can be earned through online study, through credit-by-exam, and through transfer from other four-year schools (in cases where one of the profiled institutions has limited offerings for a particular major).

At Excelsior's current undergraduate tuition of approximately $350 per credit hour, a student requiring 60 credits to graduate could expect to pay roughly $20,000, with fees and books being extra. So the total cost of a bachelor's degree, earned through a combination of courses from a community college and Excelsior, would be less than $40,000. In fact, most Excelsior students pay considerably less, as they supplement coursework with credit from various forms of prior learning assessment.

When you compare costs of one program with another, be sure to look at the total cost to attain a degree, not just the per-credit amount. One factor that can confuse these comparisons is that some programs are quoted in quarter hours (2–3 month academic terms) while others are quoted in semester hours (3–4 month terms). Quarter-hour tuition is typically lower than semester hours, but more hours are required to complete a degree (180 vs. 120).

A second factor that makes comparisons difficult is that most traditional institutions require that a minimum amount of coursework be done in "residency." This doesn't mean you have to be physically on campus, but that work has to be done with that particular institution. The usual expectation is 30 credits, or one year's worth of work. For the student with more than 90 credits (transfer and PLA), it is possible that their degree will now cost more than if all of their prior work was accepted and they paid a higher per-credit tuition for the final work. Here is an example of how this might work:

	Institution A	Institution B
Tuition Rate	$350 per credit hour	$300 per credit hour
Credit Offered	100 credit hours	100 credit hours
Credit Accepted	100 credit hours	90 credit hours
Remaining Work	20 credit hours	30 credit hours
Total Cost	$350 x 20 = $7,000	$300 x 30 = $9,000

In addition to the community college transfer strategy, there are many other combinations that can help reduce the cost of degree completion. For instance, John's wife completed her undergraduate work as an adult through a combination of transfer work from both community colleges and four-year state institutions. Having satisfied the requirements for admission with this transfer work, she was admitted and graduated from the University of California, Berkeley. She then went on to earn her master's degree from Stanford University's *incredibly inexpensive*, part-time MLA program.

That all degrees are not equal in value shouldn't come as a surprise. A bachelor's degree from a relatively unknown institution with an open-enrollment policy, whereby anyone who meets basic criteria is allowed admission, does not carry the same weight as one from a brand-name private or public research university. There is no question that those who graduate from prestigious institutions see doors open more easily — and that means, of course, that those doors will remain closed for many others. This brand recognition and suggestion of specialness is part of what students receive for the very high tuition charged by the name institutions.

Nonetheless, we maintain that this brand value is greater for the traditional-aged student who is just starting a career than for the experienced adult who already has a support network of colleagues and friends and a deeper résumé of work experience than recent college graduates.

Regardless of your ultimate path and your decision to go for brand or not, the points to recall are:

1. Compare programs — as to cost, acceptance of credit earned elsewhere (or PLA), number of courses/credits that have to be done in "residency."
2. Contain costs, if this is important for you, by steering toward lesser known institutions, satisfying lower division requirements through community college or PLA work. Consider credit-by-

examination if you are well versed in a particular subject or are a good independent student

3. Weigh the value of brand against your career objectives. Remember that many relatively unknown institutions have excellent programs.

4. Look for truly adult programs. Evening or online versions of on-campus programs may or may not have the flexibility and support services you want/need.

At a time when each of us is bombarded with more information in one year than our grandparents received in a lifetime, it is not realistic to think that we can interpret and fully understand our work with the learning and skills that we developed decades ago. In fact, if we want to remain relevant and competitive, we must start to think of ourselves as lifelong learners. America needs adult learners with the courage to return to higher education to attain the skills and knowledge needed for both the defense of democracy and the continued growth of our economy.

–9–

Chris Kilgus:
Lessons Learned

One population often overlooked in higher education discussions is an essentially invisible one: those in America's prisons. As The New York Times reported in April 2008: "The United States has less than 5 percent of the world's population. But it has almost a quarter of the world's prisoners." We have approximately 2.3 million people behind bars, and if we do not offer them effective rehabilitation or education, we can expect a high rate of recidivism. Chris Kilgus offers us a unique look at why he became imprisoned and how education offered him a way to stay out.

This is a story people may not want to hear, because I committed some crimes and I spent time in jail and maybe they don't think an ex-con has much important to say. But jail's how I learned about Excelsior twenty years ago, and that changed my life.

I had been in Florida, awaiting sentencing. One thing led to another, and I wound up in Santa Cruz, California, using an assumed name. After they found me, they put me first in a pretty nice jail in San Jose. It was clean. I was in my own little world. I had plenty of books. I didn't know what else to do, so I started working out and trying to eat well, trying to meditate. I'm always a person who, when

I'm stuck somewhere, will make the best out of it. It's just my nature. But after a week of getting comfortable, the guards came for me in the middle of the night. They took me to San Francisco and threw me in the county jail. There were about fourteen people in a ten-man cell—people smoking and everything. I'm not prejudiced, but being in there with thirteen brothers made me the odd-man-out. It was a despicable jail, and a disgusting cell.

I'll never forget the night I walked into that jail. I arrived at two in the morning, and it was so dark that all I could see were filth and too many people crowded together. And the place smelled like a sewer. I remember thinking, *Okay, here's your destiny for a while.* Then all of a sudden, this little white guy I hadn't seen at first jumped up and ran over to me, and I was pretty glad to see him. With only two white guys, we were kind of forced together. Turned out, he had a degree in chemistry, and he had just gotten busted on a huge LSD sweep. He had been making tons of the stuff. There was Timothy Leary, and then there was this skinny nerd—he was number two.

Turned out he was pretty smart, and I was happy to have somebody to talk to. There was nothing else to do, so we talked for the next 24 hours. Well, after a while, I got into my concerns about my future, and I told him, "I wish there was some way I could finish my degree while I'm in here."

He said, "You can."

"No way," I said.

"Way! Come here."

You usually keep all your personal items under the mattress in a place like that. I walked over to his mattress, and he grabbed the edge of it and he pulls it back like you would pull the sheet off a body in the morgue—bam, all of a sudden. And there were all these books and catalogs and pamphlets—the whole gamut of college course materials for adult students, including *Bears' Guide For External Learning.* That may have been replaced by sites on the web now, but this was 20 years ago. *Bears' Guide* went through all the nontraditional, external learning procedures that existed and the ups and downs of all of them. Regents College was in there. That's what it was called before the name was changed to Excelsior. Here was this catalog amid a bunch of others, and this guy handed it to me. I went, "Yeah, but why bother if it's not accredited?" And he said, "It is accredited!" I didn't really know what accreditation meant, but I learned quickly.

Let me go back and tell you how I ended up in that jail. I was born in 1947, so I'm kind of old. I grew up in a small town in Kentucky—Maysville—where Rosemary Clooney was born. George Clooney came up there once in a while to see his Aunt Rosemary, because she still lived in Maysville. George actually went to high school about 25 miles away, in Augusta, Kentucky, but that's off the subject. It was a great little place to grow up.

I was a ham radio operator, and I built model planes. I was like the nerdy kid. I was all about flying—I was an airplane nut. I was a good kid in high school, and I joined the Navy Reserve, because I couldn't wait to get into the Navy and fly planes. That's how gung ho I was about joining the military. I graduated in 1965 and went on to the University of Kentucky. I was studying engineering. I was thrilled to be in college, looking forward to being a Navy pilot.

I thought everything was okay until my sophomore year in college, when I took my pre-flight test. Usually, you know, eyesight or something like that will wash somebody out. I didn't know it, but I had a hearing loss that they discovered, and that disqualified me to fly for the military. That was it for me, and I felt like I had nothing to look forward to after that.

When I got to college, I went wild. I started out okay, but I got behind the eight ball because my high school didn't really prepare me well enough. I didn't have calculus or advanced math courses. I was fairly bright, though, so I did well the first semester, and I even did okay the second semester. Then I just started running with a fraternity and drinking too much and hanging out off campus. Somebody had been telling me what to do my whole life, and suddenly I was free, and I lost it. I didn't make my grades the third semester. So

I went to another school for a while. But if I couldn't fly for the Navy, I just didn't care about school. I took off on my motorcycle. I didn't even drop my courses; I just left. The good news was that I had completed three semesters of college work, and that stays on your transcript.

This was when they had the draft, and now the Navy was breathing down my neck. I had joined the Navy Reserve to stay out of the draft, and they wanted people for active duty. At that point, I didn't want to go. If I couldn't be a pilot, I didn't want to be in at all, but they were chasing me. Remember, this was the '60s: things were getting really bad in Vietnam, and they needed all the able-bodied guys they could get. But why would I want to go to Vietnam? I tried to get lost but, you can't really get away from them. I was young and dumb about the world. I figured they would catch up with me sooner or later. I was working, and they eventually tracked me down. They didn't arrest me. They just wanted me to go on active duty, and I couldn't get out of it.

So, like a lot of other young guys, I took my physical and lied on all the physical afflictions that I could—back pain, headaches, dizzy spells—none of which worked. I married my girlfriend the day before I went on active duty, because I thought for sure that I was going to Vietnam, or onto some ship supporting troops in Vietnam— something horrible like that. But they sent me to Whidbey Island, Washington. It was totally beautiful. I was stationed at the naval air station there. I was still mad that I couldn't fly, and there I was, working on airplanes.

I got through it, though. I only had to do two years, and I was on the *Enterprise* for a while, which was actually pretty exciting. When I got out of the Navy, my wife was pregnant, and pretty soon we had a little boy. We were living in Phoenix, Arizona. I went out and got my pilot's license on my own. I was determined to get it. I bought a little plane and rebuilt it in the back yard.

After six months there, a neighbor, whose wife was a Mexican national, approached me with an interesting proposition. Next thing

I knew, I rented a Cessna and flew down to Mexico and picked up thirty pounds of pot. I brought it back and sold it, and then I did it again the next weekend. I bought a brand-new Kawasaki 900 motorcycle, and I thought, *Wow, this is pretty good.* Remember, this was back in the 1970s, when it seemed like everybody was smoking pot. Sure, it was illegal, but we were all young, and nobody I knew thought hauling marijuana back from Mexico was the same as dealing hard drugs. There were songs about the Free Mexican Air Force. We were probably too naïve, but we weren't trying to hurt anybody.

I was back in school at this point. I was going to Arizona State, and I was taking my calculus core, and I was taking all the engineering subjects—those brutal ones, like statistics, dynamics, material science, differential equations, and circuits courses. I was actually doing pretty well. I was in electrical engineering, so I had to take a series of circuits courses—1, 2, 3, 4, 5, 6—it just keeps going. I was enjoying school until I got a taste of the smuggling thing.

One thing led to another, as it always does, and maybe three years later, about 1976, I got caught with a DC-3 full of 5,000 pounds of marijuana. That's a huge plane—a 30-passenger airliner. I kept getting offers to fly bigger planes, and I couldn't stop. I tried to, but people in the business would find me and give me lots of money and bigger planes. Once you're known, they can find you. They'd show me a plane, and I'd go, "Oh my god, an Aero Commander," and next thing you know, I was flying that thing around, making lots of money. It was really the adventure, and the flying, that I loved most.

But I did get caught, of course. I went to trial, and we all just threw money at it. There were all kinds of people involved. There were seven people on the ground to meet the load—5,000 pounds is a tremendous amount—and then myself and another guy in the plane. We all ran here and there, but they finally caught us. When they called the case in court, about 30 people stood up—all the defendants, their lawyers—and we just started dragging it out, driving the federal judge nuts. We had the best lawyers, and they were using every technique to delay it. Finally, we came to the conclusion that we would just work it on appeal. "If you plead guilty, we will let you stay out on appeal," they told us. So we pled guilty. I got five years, and I was immediately out on appeal. I moved to Colorado to hide out, in case the appeal didn't go my way.

In the meantime, once I wasn't being a pilot, I fell right back into being an engineer. I was going to the University of Colorado, taking engineering courses. I was an engineer without a degree, and there was a stigma around that. I continued trying to get my degree, but it was a long process. You can't make the same money, and you're always explaining that you're an engineer but you don't have a degree to prove it, even though you have a lot of experience. It gets to you. I wanted to get my degree, because I had already invested a whole lot in my education.

Let's see, by then it was the end of the '70s, and I was working. I had won the court case on appeal, on a technicality, and I was free again. I got a great job—I was working for the National Center for Atmospheric Research in Boulder, Colorado. I wasn't flying the plane, but I was on a plane. It was one of those storm chasers, and we were flying it all over the world. It was damn exciting. By then, I was divorced and had a new girlfriend. She hated me being gone so much, and it didn't pay all that well. We were always low on money.

I was still working this great job when a friend found me. He made me an offer for one run to Mexico. It looked like a sure thing, and I tried it, but I crashed because the runway wasn't long enough. They used metric instead of "American" to measure the runway length—a mistake that NASA had also made at one time. They crashed a spaceship into Mars instead of landing on it. The Mexicans made the same mistake when they were building their jungle runway.

It took me a week to get home. I was torn up pretty bad, and I told my girlfriend I'd never do it again. But two weeks later, the guy was back again. And he was going, "Okay, this is the plane, and we're going to Colombia. Look at the money we can get." And I said,

"Okay," even though I had told my girlfriend that I wouldn't do it. The flying and the money and the adventure were just too much temptation for me, and they cost me way too much in the end. I should have known better by that time.

So there I was again, flying a plane to Colombia, where I was immediately arrested and thrown into a Colombian prison. I was freaked out at first, but it turned out okay because we had money. A cab would bring us food from restaurants every night. I had a water dispenser. They'd bring me bottled water, and I could get my clothes washed. It was just fine. There were a lot of other pilots and sailors in there—Americans—that the government had snatched up. Nobody got out except for me. I don't know how, but by some miracle, my connections got me out in a month. I even got my plane back, and I flew it home. It was crazy.

Pretty soon, I was flying to Colombia every couple of weeks—bigger and bigger planes, but still just marijuana. No cocaine. I was really opposed to that; I think there's bad karma with that. Everybody I knew who was associated with coke ended up getting killed. Marijuana was all I was interested in. I just loved flying those big, heavy planes. I was in a giant Lockheed, like the one that Howard Hughes flew around the world—like the one that Amelia Earhart tried to fly around the world. A Lockheed Lodestar, it's called; we had one of those. I had approximately 5,000 pounds on board when, somehow, the DEA tracked us out to our landing site in Florida. Third time was definitely not a charm in my case. This was five years after my first arrest, but it was the same charge as before—except this time it was the state of Florida, not the federal government.

All of us who got arrested tried to drag it out again, but the state of Florida wasn't going to play any games with us. They wanted to give me five years, and that's all there was to it. So when it looked like it was our last chance, three of us jumped bail and got the hell out of Florida. That's how I landed in Santa Cruz. I took an assumed name; I got a job as an engineer at Plantronics Electronics—the headset manufacturer—and I started living another life. I bought a house and went straight for eight years. Then, all of a sudden one morning, federal agents kicked in my door. That was in 1990.

Now we're back to where this story began. As I sat there in that San Francisco jail cell, reading about Regents College, I could see they were accredited and working through the University of the State of New York. All the credits I had from the University of Kentucky were going to transfer, and I could earn an accredited degree. As I read the materials, I realized the key was to find the right courses to take. I did my own self-assessment from their guidelines, and it turned out after all those years of taking courses here and there, that I was within three courses of getting a bachelor's degree—not in electrical engineering, but a bachelor of science degree. All those electrical engineering courses counted as electives, and the remaining courses I needed were physics courses, which I could take at a distance. I realized, right there in that smelly jail cell, that I didn't have to waste the time I knew I had to spend in prison. I knew I had screwed up, and here was something I could do about it. I could give my life some purpose if I went back to school. That changed everything.

So, after my short stay in San Francisco, I was sent back to Florida. I went before the judge, and he gave me two years instead of the five, because marijuana was no big deal at that point. All this time had gone by, and I had kept my nose clean. But I had to do the two years, no getting out of that. I served my time all over the country— Florida, Oklahoma, California, Arizona. It's called diesel therapy: they just keep you on the run.

But none of that mattered. I was excited to finish my degree. I wrote to Regents and got back information that Ohio University had the distance courses I needed. They had a circuits course and, even though it wasn't for credit, I knew it would get me started again, so I took that right away. I asked for a calculator, and they let me buy one and keep it. They also let me buy stamps and write as many letters as I wanted. I can't complain about how the system treated me.

By now, I had spent twelve years not taking courses, because I was on the lam. Why bother? As I jumped back into even that first circuits course, I realized that I didn't have my edge anymore. Math, chemistry, physics—they were all difficult at this point. But prisons always have decent libraries, and they end up with a lot of college textbooks. I found some older university physics, chemistry, and calculus textbooks. And I started at page one of each of them, and I went through and worked every problem in all three books.

It took me three or four months. I was just walking around, carrying those books. You wait a lot in prison. You go and you wait, and you sit, and then you wait even more. It would drive sane people nuts, but I always had a book with me. The moment I sat down, I would open it and I'd be gone—I wasn't there anymore. People would have to push me and say, "Hey, come on, let's go." We'd stop for a minute, and I'd be reading in line. I ended up highlighting the whole book. I should have just highlighted what I didn't think was important, or maybe I should have just dipped the whole book in orange highlighter. It didn't matter in the end, because I used them so much.

I want to explain something about prison. It's a truly hopeless place for inmates, a dark place full of regrets. I had a son, and with all my flying around, I wasn't there for him—not the way I should have been. It was a dangerous life, and I was removed from my family when they needed my support. To have all of that over with now is a tremendous relief in my life. If you're lucky enough to have people who care about you, you may get a visit once in a while, and that means a lot. I had a girlfriend on the outside who sent me a letter every single day, and I had my dad. He has passed away now, but he was a very conservative man. He was a pharmacist for years, and a Republican. Plus, he was a pilot in World War II, and some of the best times he had were in the war with his flying buddies. When I got my pilot's license, it was hard for him to accept how I used that license and what I did.

But I was lucky. He didn't hold onto his anger and judgment. After I went to prison, he forgave me, and his forgiveness made me realize the mistakes I had made. Then, when I told him about going back for my degree, he got on board and started to write the checks and act as the liaison to Excelsior for me.

There are things called count times in prison, and there are three of them a day in the federal system. One of them is 4:00 in the afternoon—you hear it announced over the P.A. system—and everybody has to go to their bunks to be counted. They have to account for everyone in the entire system to make sure that nobody has escaped, and you sit there until the count is cleared. Well, during that time, they come around and hand out the mail. I got a letter every single time, and I got my textbooks for school from my father, and those are the things that made my life worthwhile in there. They're what gave me hope. But there were a lot of other guys with me who never got one letter, not for the whole time I was in there.

There's real despair if you're incarcerated, and there's the matter of trying to get respect, too. You can get respect various ways: you can tattoo yourself; you can align yourself with a gang; you can be the baddest guy in there; you can be athletic—really good on the basketball court—and that worked for me. But if you're carrying around a book, and somebody happens to ask, "What's that?" And you answer, "I'm working on my degree," whether they're a fellow inmate or a correctional officer, that earns you real respect. Most people who are trying to do something positive for themselves, like get an education, will earn respect even from the most hardened criminals.

Honest to God, when I realized I could get my degree, you have no idea how that felt. I realized that, for me, it was probably the only way I was ever going to finish. I knew I'd feel too old to go back to school by the time I got out, and I would have to start over. I had proven to myself that I couldn't carry on too well without some purpose. But in prison, I didn't have anything else to do, and I got into the studying. When you learn all those things intensely, in a short period of time, it all seems to fall together in a really beautiful way—that triad of calculus, physics, and chemistry. When I learned it all over again, all at once like that, it was like fireworks going off, and I finally understood how science works. It really filled in my life.

My bachelor of science degree back then was actually issued by the University of the State of New York, and it had my name on it. It's still on my wall. I can't believe it. It was such a blessing. I immediately got a job when I got out, making $50,000 a year, in 1991. Honestly, I would never have finished my degree without that two-year stint in prison, because I would have gotten out and I would have gotten another okay job as an engineer without a degree, and with a stigma, and making a lot less money. It cost me probably 20 or 30 thousand a year in lost wages before I got my degree.

When you get out of prison, there's such a stigma when you try to get a job. "What's on your resume?" the interviewer will ask, and when you answer, "Well, I just got out of Florida State Prison, and I made furniture while I was in there," you're not going to get a great reaction most of the time. But if you could say, "I got my degree in economics while I was incarcerated," you might have a better shot at landing that job.

If you have your degree, there's prestige involved, too. You know, that's on my résumé—Bachelor of Science in Physics, University of the State of New York, 1991—and employers can call Excelsior up and they'll say, "Yeah, he's got it." That's a fantastic thing. After all the trouble I've had in my life, what a break. You know, along with getting those two years and that concentrated time to study, another thing came with it, and that was my commitment not to get in trouble again. You could beg me, offer me a Lear Jet and a million dollars, and I wouldn't fly another load. Life is a lot better now.

Finding Excelsior was just a miracle for me, and I want to pass along how fortunate I am. When I first got out of prison, I tried to start an organization called Incarcerated Students of America (ISA), to help guys go back to school and do what I had done. But that was in the early 90s, before the internet started up, and nobody I talked with wanted to help inmates do that. But I think it might work now, even though a lot of programs to help prisoners improve and educate themselves have been slashed because of budget constraints.

Here I am 19 years out of prison, and this chapter has been the first time I've told my story, and if even one person in prison reads it and changes his life because of what I've said, and what happened to me, it's going to be a fantastic thing. I'm also going to try again to get ISA off the ground as a non-profit, and that would definitely be a vehicle that could help me give something back. I owe it to my mom and dad, to my family, to Excelsior, and to anybody else who ever helped me out.

$-10-$

How Do You Find the Right Path?

Finding the right direction in life is always a challenge. During his military career, John served on seven different ships, traveling through nearly a dozen different bodies of water, and like all sailors, he was often concerned with how to get safely from point A to point B. Years later, while administering a graduate program in career development, he saw many parallels. Whether navigating through the South China Sea or through life, we need to regularly determine where we are in relation to our end goal, and consistently determine what compensations we need to make to stay on track. Just as wind, currents, and human error can push a ship off course, jobs, health concerns, family matters, and life events in general can place obstacles and challenges in your path as you work toward a college degree. If you don't pause periodically to take a fix on your progress, you may never know how far or how close you are to reaching port.

In the next few pages, we will suggest some ways to take stock of where you are now and determine where you want to go. We will focus specifically on how you can find a way to start or complete your degree, or obtain some other form of academic credential. Regardless of what some skeptics may claim, you always have more career and life options available to you with a degree than without one.

No matter where you are along your career path today—just starting off, making good progress, or seriously off-track—it could be a good time to "fix your position" and draw a new track line. To do this, it helps to know where you want to go. Often, employers ask new hires where they want to be in five years. The majority can't answer the question. They haven't given serious thought to an end goal.

There is an old adage that says, basically, *When you don't know where you want to go, any path will take you there.* For our purposes, we will assume that even if you don't know today where you want to go with your career and/or life, you accept that a college degree will help you get there, once you decide. Thus, most of this chapter will focus on getting you on the path to a degree.

As you take stock, know that it is okay not to have an exact image of where you want to be in 5, 10, or 15 years. And if you are a parent, please show this same flexibility to your children. The idea that 18-year-olds know what they want to do with the rest of their lives is unrealistic, to say the least. Often, what masquerades as initial certainty wears off during their college years. Some may become disillusioned during their early college course-work and drop out altogether. Many complete their programs as originally intended, only to change careers later, while others stay the course and spend a lifetime doing work they no longer enjoy or find meaningful. Rare indeed are those who articulate a specific path at 18 and find that their original choices provide a satisfying lifetime of work. Though no reliable data exists for lifetime career changes, career counseling statistics and the US Bureau of Labor estimate that most of us change jobs ten or more times during our working lives.

John's first career decision came from a desire to escape the farm. That he stayed 21 years with the military came from a belief in the work of the organization and in a strong feeling that he did not want to start all over economically. However, upon retirement at age 39, he had no idea what would come next and no track line to a particular future. All he knew for sure was that he needed to earn an income, and all subsequent decisions were economic, as may be the case for many readers.

As you seek the right career track, you may need to move around, try different things, and be brutally honest about what is important to you. Once you know yourself, in terms of values, skills, ambitions, and factors that bring you satisfaction, you are at a real advantage in confronting, "Where next?" For some, there doesn't have to be a "next." There are those who so enjoy what they are doing that they don't aspire to other positions or types of work. That's terrific—for them. However, even here there is a benefit to further education, regardless of whether it is for a degree. Additional coursework can add to the enjoyment of their lives and help to make a transition to what some pundits call the "Third Age"—that time which comes after childhood/adolescence and jobs/career.

Make no mistake about it, this can be difficult work. There are, however, many resources to assist with this part of the journey. One of the best, and certainly most time-tested, is a book written by Dick Bolles. *What Color is Your Parachute?* has sold more than 10 million copies, due in part to the author having refreshed the contents on a near-annual basis since its original publication in the 1970s.

The current edition of *Parachute* supports the model we have been discussing. The chapter "Where do I go from here with my life?" addresses the concept of taking stock. Chapters that follow deal with "Once you know exactly what you are looking for" and the various stages of job search and/or career change.

Knowing that going back to school can be a part of the taking-stock process, we will focus on "finding the right path to a degree." Hopefully, with the help of the aforementioned career development resources and your openness to self-reflection, including clarifying your goals for the future, you will gain clarity about your educational needs.

Going Back To School: Those words may fill you with apprehension, excitement, or both, depending upon your past experiences in the classroom. Important to remember is that going back to school today is not likely to be anything like what you experienced before, depending on how long it has been. You are probably more mature, better focused on the content of classes, and concerned with getting good value for your tuition dollar.

Many returning adult students have been out of school either since high school or since an aborted attempt at college, often for 20 years or longer. Many have lackluster transcripts and hold serious reservations about their ability to go back to school while juggling family, job, and personal life. Despite these reservations, many have gone on to become distinguished students, never giving themselves permission to earn less than an A grade. Others, unfortunately, have fallen victim to their uncertainty, and their difficulties with such initial challenges as establishing a routine, obtaining family buy-in, or writing an essay. This serves to reinforce their belief that they are not cut out for college.

As teachers and administrators, we know how important it is to be attuned to the needs of the newly returned student. Their experiences during the first two to three terms often determine their eventual persistence and success. A little additional support early on can make a significant difference in both the confidence levels and end grades of these individuals. After the third term, even the more uncertain students have usually created support systems, routines, and expectations (both for themselves and others) that allow them to progress with greater independence and less support.

To reduce stress during this process, it helps to have a plan, something like the track line for a ship's voyage. In addition, it's not only important to have an idea about what type of academic work and credential will help move you along, but it's important to find an institution that meets your needs.

Once you have made your decision to return to school, one of your concerns will be, "What type of program do I want to enroll in?" Given the financial cost and missed opportunity associated with a poor choice, you will want to put careful thought into your selection. Questions to ask yourself may include:

- Do I want to pick up where I left off when last in school?
- Do I want to take the quickest route to a degree (where the greatest amount of my prior work will be accepted) and not worry about a particular major?
- Is there a program that will provide skills and knowledge for my current work (and possible promotion) or will aid in making a career change?
- Are there programs that will satisfy a particular interest or need for me?
- Is my prior training, experience, and education well suited to a particular program?

Once you have a sense of whether you want to focus on a particular subject area or just want to complete a broad degree that is not specific to a particular field, there will be other questions to consider:

- Do you want to earn and apply credit for corporate or military training? If so, it can save you time and money. The key is to find a program where such training can be accepted and an institution that recognizes American Council on Education credit recommendations. Luckily, most do, but to varying degrees.
- Do you understand what is meant by a residency requirement? This is where a program/institution may expect you to do a certain amount of academic work with them, regardless of the actual number of credits needed to graduate. For a bachelor's degree, it is typical for a school to require that 30 credits (10 three-unit courses), or one academic year's work, be done with them. However, some of the schools profiled in this book, including Excelsior, do not have such requirements.
- Do you want to go to school year-round, finishing in as short a time as possible?
- Can you take more than one course per term? Increasingly, adult online students are taking two eight-week courses per

academic term in succession (three credits each). This allows them to focus on one course at a time while completing two over a normal 16-week semester. This also may enable a student to qualify for "part-time" federal financial aid.

- Do you know about credit-by-exam? Adults with substantial prior learning, either from work experience or personal interest, often find that they can accumulate credits by taking approved examinations from such organizations as The College Board (CLEP), Educational Testing Service (DSST), or Excelsior College (EC or UExcel exams). In the case of Excelsior, there are over 50 subject areas to select from. In each case, passing grades on these exams can satisfy degree requirements. Those who are comfortable studying independently also find this to be an inexpensive and efficient way to earn credit.

- Do you want to study online, in a classroom, or some blend of both? Depending upon the program you select, the flexibility of your personal schedule, and your style of learning, one of these formats may be more appealing than the others:

Evening classroom programs have been around the longest and may offer the greatest variety of subject matter options. However, these are time-and-place specific, typically require commuting, and are the least flexible from a scheduling standpoint.

Online programs have gained acceptance by both employers and traditional academic institutions. Typically you study at times and places of your choosing, submitting assignments within a prescribed time frame. More and more programs are now available in this format.

Blended programs, combining some classroom and online instruction, are growing in popularity. But the cost of commuting for the classroom sessions can offset some of the online advantages, especially for those who are at a distance from the classroom site.

- Do you want to study à la carte, or as part of a group in a highly structured program? If you only need a few courses to finish your degree, you will likely want the freedom to pick and choose. However, if you need 60 units or more (two years worth of work), you may want to start a prescribed program that gives you a set schedule and a fixed curriculum (either online or in a classroom). This provides greater predictability and can take a great deal of stress out of the process, at least for some. A fixed cohort program, whereby you study with the same group through the entire curriculum, works well for some people, as classmates help each other succeed. Experience has shown that "virtual cohorts," where students do not meet face to face, can be just as cohesive as more traditional formats.

- How much are you prepared to spend to earn a degree? For those who say "as little as possible," you should be prepared to work with an institution such as those profiled in Chapter 6, which can help assess where you are, what credits you still need, and the various available options for filling in the needed work. Through a process of "aggregation" you can have prior training and experience assessed for possible credit. Other forms of prior learning or independent study can be evaluated through the exams mentioned above. Finally, when presented with a list of courses that still need to be completed, those that satisfy general education requirements can typically be taken at a local community college, where tuition is most reasonable. Upper division, or courses for a major, will need to be taken from a four-year institution, at the 300 or 400 level of course numbering.

As a general rule, public institutions are less expensive than private schools. However, there are exceptions. If you apply to a public institution in a state other than the one in which you reside you may be asked to pay the "out of state" rate of tuition. This is often several times higher than what is charged for "in state" students and may be as much as some private institutions.

While Excelsior is a private institution, its tuition is not much higher than that of many public ones. Additionally, given its generous transfer policies, acceptance of prior learning and exams, and minimal "residency" requirement (4 credits), the total cost of a degree is frequently much less than those with lower tuition rates but higher residency requirements. When comparing program costs, it is a good idea to compare the total out-of-pocket cost (tuition, fees, and books) of one program against the other. Per credit rates alone can be quite misleading.

Cost, of course, isn't everything. Program availability probably comes first. If the low-cost institution doesn't have the program you want, there is little to be saved. Also, finding a program that fits your lifestyle may be more important than total cost. Convenience has value.

Another concern may be brand name. Graduating from a well-known, prestigious institution can carry value in its own right. Such schools often enjoy name recognition that can open doors or place your résumé at the top of the stack. For some, however, the limited offerings and greater cost of these adult programs are not worth the cachet. Again, other program features or individual needs may shift the balance toward lesser-known, yet still well-regarded schools.

If you have gone through the process of life and career assessment and thought about the type of academic program you want, it's time to select a school. Before actually doing so, however, there are a few rules you need to understand:

- You should only consider a regionally accredited institution. There are six regional accrediting bodies: New England, Middle States, Southern, Western, North Central (a.k.a. Higher Learning Commission), and Northwestern Commissions on Higher Education. While there are national accrediting bodies, their forms of accreditation are generally considered as secondary to regional. Accreditation is important because credentials from non-regionally accredited schools are often not recognized for purposes of licensure, some forms of employment, or to meet requirements for an advanced degree. Remember John's experience in Chapter 5. The lack of accreditation left him with a useless credential and $1,200 poorer. There are many online institutions that claim forms of accreditation that are non-existent or from sham organizations. Regional accreditation is your assurance of legitimacy.

- Cheaper doesn't necessarily mean better. As with any product or service, you usually get what you pay for. If the only feature of a program that appeals to you is its price, it may not be right for you. Consider price along with all the other program aspects we have discussed.

- More expensive doesn't necessarily mean better. Again, the program, its format, the institute's reputation, its willingness to accept credit from prior learning, and overall student support should be evaluated along with the cost. Ask what it is that you are getting in benefit for a higher cost.

- Online learning is not of poorer quality than that found in the classroom. In 2009 the US Department of Education released a study showing that, with online and blended formats, students learn at more rapid rates than in a classroom setting.

- Online learning is not easy. Many for-profit institutions have sold online programs with an over-emphasis on convenience. This has translated in the minds of some students as "easy." This is not the case and partly explains the higher drop-out rates for online students (who find that the reality isn't what they expected).

- All online programs are not the same. Some institutions have taken their inventory of "distance education" videotapes or correspondence courses and converted them to online delivery. This has produced mind-numbingly boring "electronic correspondence courses" and/or talking head videos with e-mail course assignments. Neither format is particularly interactive or engaging. At the other end of the spectrum are media rich courses addressing multiple learning styles that are highly interactive and leave the student wanting more. Thus, when someone tells you they like or hate online programs, it is important to know about the use of media, the level of instructional design and the rates of student completion.

The classroom is great for those who want structure, face-to-face interaction, and the opportunity to satisfy social as well as academic needs. Online, on the other hand, tends to be better suited to those who require flexibility in their study patterns and who do not do well with the dominant classroom activity: listening to lectures.

Don't get fooled by the "practitioners vs. theorist" model of instruction. Some institutions tout that your instructors will be practitioners who are still active or recently retired from the field in which they are teaching. They are "products of the real world who know how to put theory into action." These instructors, who are almost always part-time, are contrasted with the typical academic types who can teach theory but have never put it into practice. The not-so-subtle implication is that the latter adds little of value to your learning experience. Nothing could be further from the truth. A truly outstanding program is going to provide both. Yes, you want the practical "how to" perspective. However, you also need the theory and new knowledge that comes from a full-time faculty/researcher. One without the other is likely to provide suboptimal learning.

What is most important about an institution's faculty is their ability to teach. Do not assume that someone with a PhD was necessarily born to teach, or that someone with only a master's degree is automatically less qualified. In fact, the only real connection is that the one with the doctorate may have spent more time observing the instructional process. Skill as a teacher has rarely been a requirement for a faculty position, and there is no reason to expect that a classroom instructor will actually have undergone training in pedagogy, adult learning theory, or even presentation skills.

This is not the case online. Nearly all of the most highly regarded online programs require their faculty—practitioner and theorist alike—to undergo training in online instruction. Some of these programs are up to a month in length and are a condition of employment. Additionally, the online environment allows program administrators to monitor and evaluate the quality and frequency of student/instructor interaction to a degree not seen in the classroom.

While there are many types of institutions that serve the returning student, the most common are: public, two- and four-year; private, non-profit; and private, for-profit. Under these broad headings, there are further breakdowns. For instance, "public" may apply to community colleges, state teaching institutions, and large, flagship research universities. Increasingly, the old two- and four-year classifications are becoming obsolete as students take longer to finish a degree. And "private" extends from specialized associate-degree granting institutes and colleges to such universities as Harvard and Stanford. Within the "for-profit" world, some of the largest are online or virtual universities such as Phoenix, Kaplan and Ashford. Here are some pluses and minuses of each category:

Public, two- and four-year

Pluses: Less expensive
          Well known, no question of legitimacy
          Quality instruction (usually)

Minuses: Impersonal
          Focused on traditional student
          Rigid

Private, not-for-profit

Pluses: More personal (usually)
          Less bureaucratic (usually)

Minuses: More expensive
          May or may not be structured to serve adults
          Uneven quality of instruction (often)

Private, for-profit

Pluses: High level of convenience
Customer service
Adult oriented
Breadth of offerings

Minuses: Higher cost
Uneven instruction
Reputation (several have been accused of deceptive/high pressure marketing practices)

In summary, when selecting an institution from which to earn your degree, ask yourself these questions:

- Does it have a program that meets my needs and interests?
- Is it regionally accredited?
- Can I afford the cost?
- Will they help me with financing, such as through loans and scholarships?
- Does the instructional model fit my life? For instance, how often will I need to be in class and for how long?
- Do I want a brand name and am I willing to pay for it?
- Do I know in advance who the faculty will be?
- Can I "test drive" an online course to see if the format will work for me?

– 11 –

Shannon McMillan:
An Unrestricted Education

Following an injury that ended his dream of playing baseball, Shannon McMillan gave up on education and dropped out of college. But a series of events led him to the Navy and ultimately a bachelor's degree. Hard work and a strong support system have opened a new life for him as an unrestricted line officer within the Navy . . . and beyond.

This doesn't apply to everybody, but when you go to college as a kid, right after high school, after being in school for 12 years straight, it's a party. You're not really concerned about academics. You're there to have fun. You're there to party. But as an adult, when you go to school, it's a totally different mindset. You care if you get an A or a B. You care if you show up to class, because most of the time, you're spending your own money to get your degree. You care about going back and making sure you're getting quality. Also, you don't want to have to do it over. It's better to produce quality and do it one time. You want to get an understanding of a subject and not have to do it all over again. The mindset of an adult student is totally different than a younger one.

I was born in 1962, and I grew up in the '70s in South Carolina.

I went to a little high school in Denmark, South Carolina, graduating in a class of about 250. I graduated in 1980 and was profiled in *Who's Who Among American High School Students*, and in *Distinguished American High School Students* as well. That was for both academics and sports. You have to be well-rounded to get that. I was the captain of my high school band, too. I played the trombone and the sousaphone. I was only about 5' 4" at the time, but it was a lot of fun. Since high school, I haven't played either instrument very much, but I do sing. I've also directed church choirs. I direct and sing in a church gospel choir now. I just went to another side of music, that's all.

I went to Voorhees College, also in Denmark. I played baseball and majored in theater. In 1982, when I was a sophomore, I hurt my ankle. Baseball was my dream, but with my ankle injury, I couldn't play anymore. And when the director of the theater program decided to leave for a bigger college, I left, too.

At the time, it was really bleak. It seemed like there was nothing to do, and I was bitter about a lot of things. When my cousin came home to visit in the summer of 1983, I was working at little jobs. She said, "Hey, why don't you go in the Navy? I did it, and it's fun." I said, "Nah, I don't want to do that." But after she talked some more, we formulated a plan: I would go into the Navy as a postal clerk, do four years, get out, and go work in a post office. I could retire after 20 years, and all my benefits would be lined up. That was the plan.

So I went to the recruiting station. I'll never forget what happened. The recruiter—his name was Master Chief Heisenrider—just laughed at me when I told him my plan. First thing he said was that I had to take a test to see if I was even eligible for the Navy. "Okay, no problem," I said. "I'll take the test." I did, and afterward he sent me to the Military Induction Processing Station, where they told me, "Nope, you can't be a postal clerk." I protested—that was all I wanted to do. They told me that I was going to be in fire control, and I responded, "Nope. If I wanted to fight fires, I'd stay home. I'd go join the fire department." Then they said, "That's not what we do. In the Navy, a fire controlman starts fires. You'll be using missiles and rockets, guns and bombs, radar and computers." Now they had my attention. Then they said, "We'll give you a $1,500 bonus if you sign up." So I said, "Where are the papers?"

Well, the idea of a four-year enlistment went out the window pretty quick. I had to sign on for six years to be trained in advanced electronics. So I just shifted my dream. My plan went from postal clerk to advanced electronics. I figured I'd get out in six years with all the Navy's training and find myself a job in computers or radar or gun systems.

My first tour was four-years afloat. That was really great. I was an enlisted man and realized that the rate of chief petty officer, which is the pinnacle of the enlisted rate, was something I wanted to strive for. My second tour of sea duty, from 2005 to 2008, took me to Bahrain in the Middle East, just off Saudi Arabia. There I was weapons officer, in charge of weapons from Kazakhstan to the Red Sea. Every bullet, every weapon that traveled in and out of there, I or someone in my field had to account for.

During that time, I was mentoring some of the junior sailors. One day, I walked this young lady over to the Navy campus, which is our educational office, to get her enrolled in classes. When we got over there, I was looking through some pamphlets while I was waiting, and that's when I happened upon Excelsior College's brochure.

As I looked through it, I thought, *Wow, I already have some college credit, and I'm already doing some of this stuff anyway.* So I gave them a call and talked to one of the counselors. She said, "We need your transcripts, and we need to see where you are right now. We'll determine how many credits you're still going to need." I did that, and the information that came back was awesome. The college's assessment said I was four or five classes away from an associate's degree, depending on which way I went—for my AA or my AS. Then they also told me what I'd need for a BA or BS degree.

I got really excited about that, and the first thing I did was take two classes. I'm not really sure why I took two classes to start with. Maybe I was just feeling over-zealous. The first time I turned in a paper, the instructor sent it back to me and said, "I know this is not your best work." I was like, "Wow." That kind of shocked me. But that was also the last D for an assignment that I received — everything after that was As.

That grade woke me up, and you know what? I thank that instructor more because she sent the paper back to me than if she had just passed it and given me an A, because it made me think, *Hey, this is something you need to pay attention to. This is not something that's fly-by-night. You really need to focus and buckle down.* At the end of her class, her B was the only one that I received, but that B was probably my best grade. The As, yeah, I worked hard for them, but I had to really work to get that B.

I had always wanted to finish my degree, and I had been taking classes — one class here, and then maybe two years later another class, and then three years after that maybe another. But I never put anything together to create a road map for a degree. When I saw Excelsior's brochure, something about it just made me want to call. It captured my attention. Everything flowed. Nothing was hidden. When I did call, it was like the counselor knew who I was. She spoke to me like she actually cared about whether I got my degree or not. That was very important to me.

After I enrolled and got things going, every time I called the school and spoke to one of the counselors, they always sounded like they knew what was going on. Everything was documented. I never spoke to the same person more than three times, and I never spoke to the same counselor twice, back to back. Say I spoke to Barbara on Tuesday, and then Shirley on Thursday — well, Shirley sounded like she had been talking to me on Tuesday. They never made me feel like, "Oh, she told you this but she's not here today, so you'll have to call back." I never got that. It was always, "Oh, sure, we understand. We have this, and we can offer you that. If you do this, then we can get you here." It was always like I was the only student at Excelsior. That's the way they made me feel. From then on, I just kept telling all my junior sailors, "Hey, we've got to get you enrolled in school, and Excelsior is a very good one. This is what they've done for me. Let them evaluate your transcripts and see what they'll do for you."

I was nervous about going back to college. However, after those first two classes and receiving that D, I was hungry. I couldn't wait until the next class was over so I could enroll in another one. The first time I got hit with a major paper, it had to be in American Psychological Association (APA) format. When I left school in 1982, I certainly hadn't been using APA format. I wasn't researching anything. So I had to find out how to punctuate and how to cite the works I used. But once I got it, I was even hungrier to know more. I wouldn't allow myself to get anything less than an A. I made myself do whatever work I had to do to earn it. I didn't want to send anything half-done to my instructors. They worked hard for me, and I didn't want them to feel I had let them down.

I was nervous about school. It had been over 20 years since I had been in a college. I was afraid of the new—what else was out there that was new and different? Could I de-program myself to not be the expert? Could I adapt and go into "learn mode?" During my 20 years in the Navy, I had been teaching. I had been giving the instruction. I had been mentoring. I had been the person sailors would come to and ask, "Chief, I don't know how to do this. Can you show me what to do here?" I had been their go-to guy.

But now, I would be the student, and I wasn't sure if I knew how to do that again. I knew I could listen. I could follow instructions. I could follow orders. That's easy. They tell you to go, you go. But to be a student, and to have to dig, to have to think, to have to put down on paper and articulate to someone who may know absolutely nothing about you—that could be tough. I would have to tell them in a way that they could understand. I was really nervous about that. I worried about whether my writing was going to be good enough to answer questions and get my point across. To think that someone else was going to be checking my paper and evaluating me made me very anxious.

However, once I got that bad grade, I went to work. I found out that I could make As, and I learned how to do research. I got greedy for knowledge. I wanted to know more. I wanted to find out more.

I started with Excelsior in 2006, and the conferral for my Associate in Liberal Studies was 2007. I had a lot of credits to transfer toward my AA because of my time at Voorhees College. Also, when I had gone to school for advanced electronics, the curriculum had been evaluated by the American Council on Education (ACE). The courses I had taken had all been ACE-reviewed. Some of them carried three credit hours, some only one credit hour, and some none at all.

Many schools will take all the credits recommended by the ACE guide of reviewed programs. Excelsior is one of the schools that will evaluate Navy credits and then determine how many can be applied toward a degree. Through that process, I found that I was much closer to my degree than I thought.

After I finished my associate's, I went on to earn my BS degree in Liberal Studies with concentrations in Management and Homeland Defense. That was in 2009. Well, 25 years later, I'm still in the Navy, and I love it. I went in as enlisted, and now I'm an officer. I started as an enlisted fire control technician, and I went all the way up to chief petty officer. From there, I received my commission as a limited duty officer. As a limited duty officer, you're a commissioned officer, but you're still a technical expert. Of course, mine was in advanced electronics, guns, and missiles.

As an enlisted person, I had some really good tours and I had a lot of good mentors. A lot of great people took care of me. That's why I stayed so long. They made sure I knew things that I probably wouldn't have learned otherwise. Thanks to people who helped me and pointed things out to me, I was able to receive many commendations and recognition as an enlisted man. All of this helped with my receiving a commission.

Currently, I'm in Surface Warfare Officer's School in Newport, Rhode Island. This is where the Navy sends its officer tacticians before they go afloat. This is a big deal for me, given my background coming up through the ranks. I'm really enjoying this experience. The important point is that I'm a limited duty officer. A limited duty officer is a technician. However, the Navy also has unrestricted line officers—your traditional officers—guys who went through four years of college and Navy ROTC or the Naval Academy. When they graduate with their four-year degree, they are eligible to be commissioned as officers. They are not "limited" in terms of their careers. They can go all the way to admiral, and even aspire to chief of naval operations. They can command a ship. As a limited duty officer, you can't do that.

Since getting my degree from Excelsior, I have become aware of a Navy program where, if you obtain your bachelor's degree, you can petition to be re-designated as an unrestricted line officer. The Navy takes your degree and matches it to your military record. If you meet the criteria, you can be re-designated. I happen to be one of five who was re-designated this year. So here I am, in a school for unrestricted officers.

Right now, I have a great future. I have 25 years in the Navy. As an unrestricted line officer, I can do 30 years of commissioned service. That puts me in a position where I can actually stay in the Navy long enough to obtain the rank of captain and, hopefully, command a ship. What I really want to do is command at sea.

I have an officer friend who is also going to school and finishing his degree. Together, we have created a scholarship fund for high school seniors. It's a book scholarship for those who are going on to college. So far, we've only given away six scholarships—$500 each—$250 per semester, for books. But we're going to continue this, and it's going to grow.

I'm in a situation now where I can go to a ship and actually serve as a department head. That would qualify me to become a commanding officer of a smaller ship, such as a minesweeper. Then I could apply to be captain of a larger combatant ship. I'm in a situation where I can actually see my end-goal and know it's achievable. All of this has happened because I was able to go back and get my degree. Excelsior actually gave me a new life within the Navy that I'll be able to transfer to the civilian world when I'm ready.

I have learned that people who go back to get their degrees after the age of 35 or 40 have to put a lot into it. They're raising families and they're doing their jobs, but they are not slacking on doing their homework. They're not slacking on their search for information. They're not slacking on putting forth the effort that they need to expend in order to not just pass, but to pass with a good grade. A lot of the people that I know in adult education have graduated with honors.

I didn't think I would ever graduate from college. When I was a kid, I just stopped going. I have a totally different mindset as an adult. I'm in a good place now. There have been some bumps in the road, but there have also been many peaks. I'm looking out from a mountaintop right now, and I'm loving it.

–12–

The Last Word

America's entire system of education, from kindergarten to graduate school, needs attention. From poor test scores to the need for remediation, we are seeing the results of having taken for granted our once great system of universal education. As the world changes and becomes more competitive, young people are seeking the knowledge and skills necessary to participate in a global economy. America is under pressure to increase its intellectual capital if it is to maintain its standard of living and competitive edge.

One of the primary messages of this book is that we need to pay attention to adult learners as well as to our youth. While much attention, debate, and resources are being devoted to the traditional-aged students, only recently have we awakened to the fact that this is not enough. We cannot attain President Obama's goal of increasing graduation rates by 60% if we only focus on the next generation.

America needs to find ways to attract working and unemployed adults back to school. Depending upon which numbers you use, there are between 50 million and 90 million adults with some college education but no degree. In addition, we have millions more who have no college at all. Of these, some 23 million do not even have a high school diploma. This group, sadly, is growing by nearly one and a half million high school dropouts per year.

Going back to school as an adult is not easy. Work, family, and the responsibilities of modern life all have a claim on our time. Additionally, fear and doubt must be overcome: "Will I embarrass myself by going back into an environment where I wasn't particularly comfortable the last time?"

As we hope our research has shown, you can expect a good deal of company, both in going back to school and in wrestling with the issues of self-doubt. For those adult-serving institutions that we profiled in Chapter 6, the average age of students is late 30s to early 40s. These institutions know what it is like to juggle multiple responsibilities while working simultaneously to gain confidence in your abilities and to feel that you can be successful.

Throughout this book, we have used Excelsior College and its graduates to offer various examples. It is important to note, again, that this work isn't just about one institution. Where you ultimately choose to complete a degree is a very personal decision. Any of the institutions profiled here can provide you with the structure, guidance and encouragement necessary for success. Excelsior and Empire State were created at the same time, by the same people, in 1971. They were followed very quickly by Thomas Edison and Charter Oak. In the 1990s, they were joined by another non-profit adult-serving institution, Western Governors University, which is pioneering a variety of new forms of prior learning and competency assessment. All five of these institutions are helping to meet the education needs of working adults and are demonstrating the validity of new approaches to learning. To many, they represent the university of the twenty-first century.

In considering a decision to go back to school, it may be necessary to deal with the doubts of those around you. There are many who question the value of education and claim it is not worth the effort. Even America's media, with its fixation on college costs and student indebtedness, can give you reasons to hesitate. If this should happen, re-read Chapter 8. Ask yourself why someone with an undergraduate degree is considered for jobs and promotions that aren't available to those without a degree. Also, why are they likely to be paid more and have more stable employment? Put yourself in the shoes of an employer. Do you want someone working for you who has lots of practical experience but lacks the education to do complex problem-solving or do research and conduct analysis? Or would you prefer someone who has both experience and education and has shown that they have the skills and determination to obtain both simultaneously? In a world that is changing as fast as ours, we all need to be thinking about what skills and knowledge we will need in the next phase of our life. With the rapid changes we see in entire industries today, the need to be a lifelong learner has never been greater.

The profiles we have included here are of people who realized the connections between learning and life success, whether defined in terms of economics or personal satisfaction. These stories represent remarkable persistence, courage, and accomplishment. In another sense, they show ordinary, working adults who have discovered ways to reintroduce learning into their lives. Some struggled to balance the obligations of childcare, military service, or other professions with the demands of coursework and testing. Others returned to education later in life, with a wealth of personal experience and occupational savvy in hand, so they could change the directions of their lives and pursue new opportunities. All shared a desire for knowledge. Many had to overcome substantial challenges. None ever stopped dreaming of what they could be. These are representatives of the courageous learners who, despite the doubts and fears that can come with the unknown, are willing to risk time, money and the skepticism of others to create a better life for themselves and for others.

Our country, our communities, our families, and our collective future are dependent upon our ability to attract and support more courageous learners. While not always free of obstacles, the path to education is one well worth taking.

Appendix A

For Adults Only:
15 Essential Questions

1) *Why complete a degree? What is the benefit?*

Degrees validate educational attainment and personal development. Employers use degrees to determine suitability for positions within their organizations. Degree holders tend to make more money (significantly more in some cases) than those without. For instance, the College Board, using Bureau of Labor Statistics (BLS) data, reports that those with an associate's degree earn more than 1.28 more when compared to someone with "some college" or only a high school diploma. For those with a bachelor's degree, this grows to 1.61 (College Board data). Additionally, those with degrees are less subject to unemployment during times of economic downturn. Statistics from the BLS show that while national unemployment stands near 10% (2010), for those with a degree it is less than 5% (between 4.7 and 4.9).

2) *What is the difference between a degree and other types of credentials?*

Higher education awards four levels of degree—associate's, bachelor's, master's and doctorate, of which there are two types—PhD, or doctor of philosophy, as well as the professional doctorate—MD,

JD, and EdD. Each of these involves study in a specific subject area, such as business, engineering, history, math, etc. Some institutions, such as community colleges, only award associate's degrees. What are sometimes referred to as "four-year schools" typically award bachelor's and master's degrees. Major research universities and some four-year institutions award the doctorate, in addition to bachelor's and master's degrees.

In addition to academic degrees, there are a variety of certificate programs. Some are offered by colleges and universities and some by commercial training providers. All tend to be relatively short and very focused on a specific subject area—examples include project management, various forms of software development, a particular area of IT, negotiation, or other areas of professional development. Such certificates can lead, in some cases, to a professional designation—such as Project Management Professional (PMP) or Microsoft Certified Software Engineer (MCSE).

Degrees are usually required to advance to more senior positions, with broader areas of responsibility. Experience, plus a degree, is often the desired combination of qualifications for employment or advancement.

3) *Where should I go to obtain a degree or certificate? Aren't they all the same?*

Degrees, certificates, and the institutions that offer them all differ in various ways. In making a decision about a particular program or provider there are several questions you will want to ask (both the prospective provider and yourself). Here are a few:

- Does the program offer the subject matter I need?
- What do I want to do with the credential once earned?
- How much time and money am I prepared to invest?
- Is the institution regionally accredited? (Crucial if seeking a degree)

- Who do you know who has completed this program? Were they pleased with the experience? What has the credential (degree or certificate) done for their career?

Don't be tempted to take the cheapest or easiest program. We usually get what we pay for, and cheap or easily obtained credentials may not be seen as valuable by those making hiring/advancement decisions. Also, do not confuse "convenience" with "easy." A program may be easy to access, but that does not mean that the coursework is not rigorous. This is especially true with online programs.

Name-brand colleges and universities offer programs leading to degrees and certificates. However, these are often not designed with the adult student in mind. Lesser known providers may offer greater convenience. They may also provide more balanced forms of instruction (applied and theoretical). Individual students will need to weigh the value of name recognition against the need for convenience and flexibility.

4) *What is the big deal about accreditation?*

Accreditation is important for at least two reasons—as an indicator of quality and for entitlement to federal financial aid. In the first instance, colleges and universities agree to meet specified standards in the delivery and support of the programs they offer. The degree to which they comply with these standards is evaluated by periodic peer reviews and the examination of procedures, systems and records related to the standards. Only those institutions holding either regional or national accreditation are eligible to offer federal financial aid to their students. Unlike systems in other parts of the world, regional accreditation is considered the more strenuous and prestigious form. National accreditation is more commonly associated with some forms of career or vocational study and is not always recognized by regionally accredited institutions, especially for credit transfer or to meet the requirement for advanced study. For instance, a state university may not recognize a degree offered by a nationally accredited institution.

There are six regional accreditors in the United States: New England, Middle States, Southern, North Central, Western, and Northwestern. Many employers insist that the programs in which their employees enroll be regionally accredited as a condition for receiving tuition assistance. Such a requirement is one means of protecting against enrollment in diploma mills or low-quality programs.

5) *What factors should I consider in selecting a school?*

Start with a Web search of programs that meet your needs. Also, look at institutions in your community. Seek additional information if you don't see what you need online. Be aware that the most aggressive providers of adult degree programs are typically online, for-profit institutions. While many of these offer quality programs, not all do. This is also true in the not-for-profit world. Things to look for include:

- Accreditation (regional is preferred).
- Acceptance of credit in transfer.
- Clear statement of program requirements, work that you will have to do (after any transfer credit).
- Cost, including fees and materials.
- How long you should expect the program to take—on your schedule.
- Institutional reputation (is it well known, and if not, what indicators of legitimacy are known?)
- Convenience.

6) *Where can I go to get answers to my questions?*

There are many resources available to assist the returning adult student. Starting with the Internet and a Google search, look for programs or institutions that may hold particular interest. Once on a website, look for contact information under the admissions icon or link. Typically, you can send an e-mail or reach by telephone. If it has been a long time since you were last in school, you may want to schedule either a telephone or face-to-face meeting where you can talk through your individual needs and concerns as well as the experience that you can bring to degree or certificate attainment.

In addition to the information that can be obtained online or in a conversation with an admissions counselor, you may also want to look for books that describe the process of going back to school. The guides prepared by Dr. John Bear have often proven helpful, especially for those considering online programs. There are a number of others, plus such websites as:

- Edamerica.net
- Acenet.edu
- Ed.gov
- Back2college.com
- Degree.net

7) *Is September the only time that I can start my degree-completion work?*

No, most institutions allow transfer students (those with prior credit) to start in any term—fall, winter, spring. In addition, many adult serving institutions, such as those online, allow for entry at virtually any time. Some cohort-based programs may only have one start per year. However, these are more common at the graduate level. For those seeking to complete an undergraduate degree, there are many options for meeting necessary requirements on a year-round basis. Guidance from an admissions counselor can help with your decision in this regard.

8) *What financial help can I expect? How do I get information about this?*

There are many forms of financial assistance. Many of these involve low-cost loans, while others take the form of scholarships or grants.

If employed, see if your employer provides any form of tuition assistance. Most large companies, unions, and government agencies do. Even if your employer doesn't have a formal program, they may offer some help if you can show how your education will benefit your work.

If you are a military veteran, there are many education support programs. Additionally, as a military spouse or dependent, a number of scholarships are available.

Stafford loans and Pell grants are two of the best known federal assistance programs. While there are limits to both, the Stafford loan is available to most students, regardless of income. Pell grants, on the other hand, are primarily available to those with lower incomes.

Most adult students can control the cost of their education by being informed about various prior learning and low-cost course options. Also, they should be aware that there are substantial cost differences between public community colleges (a great place to satisfy general education requirements) and either private or four-year public institutions. Acceptance of prior coursework from other institutions, credit for military or corporate training, and credit earned through such examination programs as those offered by Excelsior College or the College Board (CLEP) are other ways of keeping costs down.

Two final bits of advice: 1) Take advantage of the "in-state" rate offered by public institutions rather than the more expensive "out-of-state" tuition that will be charged by an institution in a neighboring state. 2) Pay attention to the "residency requirement" of the institution being considered. This is the minimum amount of work that will have to be done at a particular institution in order to receive their degree, regardless of how much credit you may have earned elsewhere. It is not unusual for a program to require a minimum of one year (30 credits) "in residence" as a condition for their degree. In some cases, this minimum requirement can significantly increase your cost of completion, even from a public institution. For instance, if you only need 15 credits to meet the typical 120 target for a bachelor's degree, it could cost you more to go to a relatively low-cost institution with a residency requirement than to a more expensive one without.

All accredited institutions will have a financial aid office that can help you determine both costs (at least for their school) and possible sources of help. Often the institution's website will offer helpful information, as well.

9) *What questions should I ask before making a final decision?*

As noted above, you will want specifics around:

- Program requirements
- Credit for prior work
- Flexibility of coursework
- Cost
- Expected time requirement (per class, per course, overall)

10) *What are my options if work prevents attending classes at specific times?*

Some institutions offer programs that can be attended in a regular classroom (evening or weekend) and online, for when your schedule prevents physical attendance. Nearly all online programs offer flexibility in that assignments can be completed at times and places convenient to you, within a specified period (one week is typical).

11) *What will an employer think if I earn a degree or certificate online?*

First, most institutions do not reflect the method of instruction on either the degree or transcript. However, a degree from one of the major online-only institutions may be recognized as a "distance" degree. Over the past several years, the Zogby polling firm has conducted periodic surveys of employer acceptance of online degrees.

In each of the past two polls (2006 and 2008) he has found that the reputation of the school is more important than the method of instruction. Employers state that a degree from a well-known institution will be accepted, even if earned online. On the other hand, an online degree from a little-known institution may be more closely examined.

12) *How can I keep the cost of completing a degree as low as possible?*

- Complete general education requirements at a local community college, or study independently to satisfy these requirements by examination. Excelsior College, the College Board, and Educational Testing Service all offer exams that if passed are recognized for academic credit and can satisfy degree requirements at a fraction of the cost for tuition.

- Seek to complete your degree at an institution that will extend credit for prior learning, including American Council on Education (ACE) reviewed military and corporate training.

- Avoid programs that require all study to be completed "in residence" (that is, at that institution). Also, be aware that all but a few institutions do require some residency. Excelsior College, Empire State, Charter Oak, WGU, and Thomas Edison are institutions with the most flexible transfer policies and the lowest residency requirements.

- To shorten the time to degree completion, consider taking courses year-round (including summer). If schedule flexibility is a concern, consider taking some or all courses online (most institutions of higher education now offer some courses online).

13) *School was no fun when I was there before. Why should it be different today?*

While it still may not be fun, many adult students report that they get great satisfaction from their coursework later in life. Their prior life and work experience, plus a deeper understanding of relationships between and among subjects, provide focus, motivation, and rewards that may have been lacking previously.

14) *How long will it take me to complete a degree?*

This varies by individual and will depend on how much prior credit you can apply in transfer. A bachelor's degree typically requires 120 semester credits of study. A traditional student will typically earn 30 credits a year by taking two 15-credit semesters per year. This can be reduced to two and one-half years by completing 15 credits on a three-semester-per-year basis (i.e. summer school). This, however, envisions full-time study of five 3-credit courses per term. Transfer credit and credit-by-examination can reduce the length of completion, even for a part-time student, if you take two courses (6 credits) per term, year-around. This is doable for most adult students and is the minimum course load to qualify for federally guaranteed student loans.

15) *Many students ask, "Why is it that I have to take courses which have no practical value for my work or life?"*

What has value and what has interest varies by individual learner. That which is valued by one can be dismissed by another. However, American higher education seeks to provide its graduates with a breadth of learning that goes beyond preparation for a particular job or career. While it is important to know that one's investment of time, energy and money can be expected to generate a return, it is important to our society that we also know something about art, history, religion, science, etc. With this breadth can come the knowledge necessary to being a more informed and capable citizen. It can also enrich one's personal as well as professional life.

Appendix B

Online Learning

Accredited colleges and universities have been offering online learning since the late 1980s. As dean of management at John F. Kennedy University, John appeared before the institution's accrediting commission—the Western Association of Schools and Colleges (WASC)—in 1986 to request authorization to deliver an MBA program through the Electronic University Network. While others, including Stanford University, were offering individual courses online, this was the first degree program to be offered by an accredited institution.

Today nearly 70% of all colleges and universities are offering online programs of one type or another. In fact, the Sloan Foundation estimates that 30% of America's 19 million degree-seeking students were enrolled in an online course in the fall of 2010. Each of the five institutions profiled in this book have substantial online offerings. As a result, adult students have the opportunity to complete any outstanding coursework necessary to degree completion in the comfort of their homes, if so desired.

In considering whether online learning is an option you want to consider, take a look at the CD that accompanies this book, Access to Learning. Here, you will find examples of online courses, as well as comments about the experience from both faculty and students.

Some things you need to know include:

1) All online courses are not the same. Some are little more than electronic correspondence courses whereby the student primarily reads the course content and then takes a series of quizzes and/or examinations. While not especially engaging, such courses can offer relevant content and more immediate feedback than was possible when lessons and grading were exchanged via the US mail. Other online programs, by contrast, reflect sophisticated instructional design, use multiple forms of media, incorporate unique exercises and activities to reinforce and test learning, and offer highly interactive simulations to demonstrate concept integration and application. Ask to preview a course before enrolling, if this is a concern to you.

2) Studying online is different than being in a classroom. The trade-off, in the eyes of many, is that you can study online at times and places of your choosing. Also, you will find yourself interacting with the instructor and other students asynchronously, via the Internet. This may take time to become comfortable. Nonetheless, we strongly recommend that you separate your feelings about going back to school from your feelings about "going online." Both are likely to make you uncomfortable at first, particularly if your last experience as a student was less than positive. Know that almost all returning adults feel some trepidation when first back in class, whether physically or virtually. By the end of the first course, however, this can be expected to go away, except for the fear that many feel when it comes to a particular subject, like statistics or calculus. Once your work and family routines have been adjusted to accommodate your time commitments as a student (and your family and co-workers come to accept it), the back-to-school experience will come to feel easier and more manageable. Be sure to give yourself this time for adjustment.

3) When studying online, there are many aspects of the experience that students come to like. Not only can you study when and where you want, you can take as much time as you need to absorb the material and be sure of your understanding. Assignments typically

must be posted by a specified deadline each week; however, you can submit at any time prior to that deadline.

4) Interaction with the instructor, fellow students and most, if not all, of the material is done online. While this may feel unnatural at first, here again the actual experience of a lesson or two will provide familiarity and comfort. Research has found that students studying online can develop just as close a bond as those in the classroom.

5) Contrary to the perceptions of some, one does not need to be particularly computer savvy to study online. Learning how to transmit attachments is probably the most difficult part of the process. But even here there will be technical staff available at the offering institution to talk you through the process. Most online programs today offer 24/7 technical support.

One of the greatest misconceptions about online learning is that it is easier than traditional classroom study. This is not the case. While studying at times and places conducive to your best learning is more convenient than showing up at a specific class site after a full day of work, nonetheless the "convenience" that many online programs tout is not the same as "easy." In fact, many online programs are even more rigorous than the classroom experience because of a belief by some faculty that they need to compensate for the fact that they are not interacting with students in person and in traditional ways. Most online programs are designed to achieve the same results as those specified for on-campus students. The means by which these learning objectives are reached is the primary difference.

If you are concerned about how you might do in an online course, go to one of the "open educational resources" sites on the Internet and take one of the free courses offered by institutions from around the world (see www.oercommons.org or www.oerconsortium.org). While you won't have the same experience as with an instructor and fellow students, you will get an idea of the potential this form of learning provides, as well as your comfort with the experience.

Appendix C

Credit by Exam

For those who have developed an in-depth understanding of a particular subject area, either through self-directed study, recreational reading, or work, there is a process to validate your knowledge and earn academic credit. By satisfactorily completing an American Council on Education (ACE) approved examination you can earn both upper and lower division undergraduate credit. This credit can then be used to satisfy specific degree-completion requirements. This, in turn, can save on the cost of tuition.

The College Level Examination Program (CLEP) of The College Board is perhaps the best known of these CBE providers. However, Educational Testing Service (ETS) and Excelsior College also have similar programs. While both CLEP and the ETS offerings are focused on lower-division, general-education exams, Excelsior, which is the pioneer in this field (offering CBE prior to the creation of the CLEP program), offers both upper and lower division exams and has the greatest inventory of titles overall.

Rather than spending several hundred dollars in tuition to take a course at a local college, more and more students are studying independently, using open courseware materials from the Internet, or testing their knowledge of subjects related to their profession or personal life. All of the CBE providers offer study guides, and Excelsior even has a practice exam for most of its offerings.

The cost of an individual subject CBE assessment is typically around $100, with prep materials and exam administration (at a testing center) being additional. The number of assessments has now grown to the point where all of the general education requirements for a bachelor's degree can be earned in this manner. Also, Excelsior now offers all of the exams needed to complete an associate's degree in business. Imagine, an accredited degree earned through self-study and examinations, for less than the cost of one year's tuition on a campus.

More information about credit-by-exam is available at the websites for Excelsior, the College Board and The Educational Testing Service. The ETS program is known as DSST.

Appendix D

One Transcript Service

OneTranscript (formerly known as the Credit Bank) is a service for those who want to consolidate multiple academic records and training credits into a single Excelsior College transcript. Whether for employment or educational purposes, this service reviews official documents from the relevant issuing authorities—other colleges/universities, the American Council on Education, the military, etc.—and combines all recognized credit into a single document. This service is intended for those who want to combine their credits for use later toward a degree, whether from Excelsior or another institution.

Specific benefits of this service include:

- Makes it easier for employers or colleges to recognize all the credit you have already earned
- Eliminates requests to multiple sources, multiple times, saving you multiple fees
- No charge for adding Excelsior College(r) Examinations (ECEs) and Excelsior College courses
- Receive a discount on the enrollment fee if you enroll into any Excelsior College degree program within one year of your initial transcript completion

OneTranscript is designed to consolidate credits from a variety of sources. Here are some examples:

- Proficiency demonstrated through examination programs:
  - CLEP(r)—College Level Examination Program(r)
  - DANTES/DSST—Defense Activity for Non-Traditional Education Support/DANTES Standardized Subject Tests
  - Excelsior College(r) Examinations
  - New York University (NYU) Language Examinations
  - IT Certification Exams from—Microsoft(r), Cisco(r), SAS(r), Oracle(r), CompTia(r), and Sun Microsystems(r)
- Business/Industry/Government Training Courses evaluated for credit through:
  - ACE—American Council on Education
  - NPONSI—National Program on Non-Collegiate Sponsored Instruction
- Military training evaluated for college-level credit by the American Council on Education (ACE)
- Traditional college courses completed through regionally accredited colleges including Excelsior College

Excelsior College's OneTranscript has proven beneficial to a wide variety of adult learners. Among those who might benefit from this service are:

- Police officers looking for advancement
- Individuals interested in becoming police academy candidates
- Teachers who need to document additional learning
- Anyone seeking job advancement/promotion/placement
- Anyone seeking college-level credit from post-traditional sources

Insights from Higher Education's Leaders

Excerpts from interviews, in alphabetical order

James Applegate

Vice President of Program Development, The Lumina Foundation

Bill Patrick: What are the major issues confronting American higher education today, and do leaders in government, business and academia see those issues differently than the majority of the general public?

James Applegate: Well, I guess, in terms of the most fundamental issues confronting higher education, I'm going to sound a little bit like I'm recounting The Lumina Foundation's Strategic Plan, because we spent a lot of time thinking about what are the critical outcomes that need to occur. First of all, and these aren't necessarily in order of importance, but I think they're all necessary pieces, higher education must redefine its relationship with its supply chain, which is the K-12 system. In all these areas I note, I'm hopeful that we're in a transition period here showing some progress. I think it's a good thing that it's perhaps more difficult to characterize higher education uniformly today than it may have been in the past. I think we are seeing, in different areas on different issues, some movement.

This partnership with K-12 would be a good example. I think you do find—more than you have in the past—the understanding that the blame game with K-12 education doesn't serve anyone's interests. If we think of them as our supply chain, we have to adopt the same kind of partnership role there that the auto industry finally figured out it needed to adopt with its suppliers. It's not blaming or coercing or firing: it's understanding that their problems are our

161

problems, and maybe some of their problems are because of us. How do we work together to address the key issues around alignment and increasing the opportunities and pathways for students to see higher education as a necessary part of their future in the K-12 system?

BP: In terms of supplying higher education, do you see that K-12 pipeline as being the primary source or just one of the feeders?

JA: Well, I think another piece of that—looking at the pipeline—is the adult learner. Obviously, that's an issue we're deeply concerned about, and I think your second question refers to the adult learner. One of the clear findings as we established this big goal and then became very serious about looking at the demographics and the data and understanding what it will take to accomplish that goal (and by the way, there's nothing like a goal to really crystallize your understanding of what needs to get done), we saw that in 30-plus states, there aren't enough young people to make it possible for those states to really get to their 60% level by 2025.

The recent Tony Carnevale report suggests that maybe there's even a greater urgency than our 2025 goal—Tony uses 2018 as a linchpin date for meeting workforce needs through attainment. His report is called "Help Wanted," and it just came out from the Georgetown Center for Education and the Workforce. It has state by state analyses, as well as the national picture, and I think it lays out the problem pretty convincingly and points to the challenges that we face. But we know, in the majority of those states, there aren't enough youth. You could scoop up every baby projected to be born in those states between now and 2025 and ensure that every one of those babies graduated from high school and went to college and came out with a degree or credential that meant something, and the states still wouldn't be where they need to be.

The other side of that is thinking about what we need to do to make ourselves accessible to success for adult learners, and even this is over-simplification. There are at least three target groups among adults. There's the very large group of college stop-outs, adults who actually made it onto campuses somewhere in this country and did not manage to come out with any kind of value-added degree or credential. They probably came out with debt, but not a degree or credential that would actually help them pay off that debt. And so that's a big group.

Drop-out or stop-out, we don't know what the right word is. We talk about returning adults; we talk about adult completion. I guess, if I were to pick one, I would choose stop-out, to indicate that they're going to come back and they're going to continue their education. I don't know how broadly that term is used, but I think for those folks who started college, hopefully they've stopped out and that at some point we can convince them to come back. It's going to take both work on the side of motivating and helping people understand why they need to come back, and it's also going to take a lot of work on the provider side to create a system that is amenable to them coming back. In fact, Lumina has recently launched a $10 million program—to which we've had enormous response—to identify programs that really can, at-scale, provide the avenues for adults to come back and complete their degrees.

The second group is the one that has high school credentials but no college. For many of them, it was not an irrational decision to stop-out after high school. There were jobs (but Tony suggests in his report, those jobs are rapidly going away), but there were jobs—good jobs—to be had, but now in this, hopefully, post-great-recession era, we're seeing rapid transitions in the workforce, such that middle-class-level, living-wage jobs for high school graduates are rapidly shrinking. So we have to think of a way to provide opportunities for them to come back and up the ante on their education.

Then the third, and obviously in some ways the most difficult group, is made up of the significant percentage of adults in this country who have no high school credential at all. They didn't make it through high school. We've been struggling with this high school drop-out issue for quite a while. As a result of that, we have a lot of people in this group. We're involved in thinking about how we can reach that group.

We must reach back out and further educate the current adult population. It's not an either/or—it's a both/and. We have to do a much better job of working with our K-12 supply chain, particularly around those groups of students that they and we have done the worst job of getting through the system—low-income, first-generation students of color.

Then there's this whole question of what the outreach mechanism to draw in the adult population is. If you think about who our partners are in that—certainly the employer community has to be meaningfully engaged in that work. We're having a lot of conversations right now to determine how we more broadly engage the employer community. At some level, with the higher-skilled jobs, there is a clear recognition of the urgency of beginning to address the skill-gap that exists. There will be new jobs, but as Tony's report points out, many of those jobs require skill sets that people don't have. There was just a piece in *USA Today* a few weeks ago about how the auto industry is trying to remake itself in light of its troubles, and there are jobs emerging. While there are certainly a lot of unemployed autoworkers, many aren't people who have the skill sets to really fill the new jobs that are emerging. I think we're going to see that same issue but in an even broader way across the economy. Employers have to be partners with us to help workers return to college and to earn more advanced credentials and degrees. Higher education has to be ready to find ways to respond appropriately to the needs of the adult learner—and that includes veterans, displaced workers, and all those workers who are still working but who are still at risk because they really aren't at the level of education that they need to succeed in the long term in this economy.

In many areas with adult learners, and certainly even with young people in the traditional pipeline, we are still trying to figure things out. In some areas, we don't know what will work, but in other areas we have a good sense of what works. It's a matter of putting the policies and the incentives in place and building the will, frankly, among key populations, to make the right things happen. We know fairly confidently, for example, that career pathways—helping students identify how what they're doing is relevant to a pathway to some career or employment—is an important piece to motivate and keep them engaged in the system. Yet these career-pathway programs have been out there for a long time, and they still haven't scaled up.

I think it's one of the challenges, from a foundation community perspective, that people have been grappling with for some time. As we confront the enormity of this task—just to take our big goal of 150,000 more degrees each year, every year between now and 2025—the issue of scaling up our programs . . . I don't really frame it that way. I frame it as scaling out effective practices. How do we scale out effective practices so that they're embodied in common practice and we're just not sitting back here creating model programs and waiting for some prairie fire to occur, but we're actually strategically thinking about scaling? That's got to be in the front of all of our minds—the enormity of the task.

We have a huge college drop-out or stop-out problem—clearly, different sectors to different degrees, and different institutions to different degrees. The reason we have all those adults out there with some college and no degree is that we have not been doing our job in higher education. I'm old, so I came up in an era of, "If a student fails, it's always on the student." They weren't prepared enough; they didn't work hard enough; they lacked study skills. But when you've got, on average, 40% of your population in higher education not making it through, and in some institutions, 50 or 60 or even 70%, then you have to take a step back and realize there is a systemic problem here, in terms of a commitment to student success. Higher education has had sort of a Teflon coating in the public view. There was a tendency to think, when students didn't make it through, even on the part of parents and students, *Well, they didn't have the right stuff or they didn't work hard enough.*

Now, I'm not saying that that isn't sometimes the case. Clearly, individuals make bad decisions, or individuals find themselves in the wrong place at the wrong time in their lives. At this level of failing students, I really think we have to look systemically at what we are and are not doing. Again, there are pockets of success out there, and I don't just mean elite institutions that have a lot of money to throw at the problem. There are areas of success where institutions are demonstrating that they can bring much higher success rates for students through implementing effective practices around the ways they teach, how they structure their curriculums, the kinds of student support services they provide, and doing it in ways that are scalable. It's not like they're just throwing money at the problem—they're redesigning the business as they're doing the work. We just need to figure out a way to get those practices more broadly looked at.

So I think the success issue is one that needs to be redefined. Now that we know (I would argue that we know) that if we do not get students to some kind of postsecondary, value-added credential or degree, that the pathway to the middle class is pretty much shut off to them. Working poor is almost certainly what they are likely to be. It puts a different obligation on us as a higher education system. Success is not an optional piece for people in their lives, and it cannot be for us.

In addition to improving higher education's work as a partner in preparing students for college and ensuring their success once we enroll them, the third major challenge (again I'm basically highlighting our strategic plan because we spent a lot of time thinking about this) is the whole productivity/quality/capacity issue. Clearly, now that the Student Aid and Fiscal Responsibility Act (SAFRA)—Obama's proposed funding for higher ed that didn't survive—has gone the way of healthcare reform and the states are in economic dire straits, we know there aren't going to be many dollars from heaven (or DC) falling in huge amounts. To say that to increase attainment, we need billions more to do the work is to abandon the work.

There are people, including Lumina, who make a good argument that state and national priorities should be changed to provide additional future resources. I agree with that. Our position is that we should be prioritizing postsecondary college achievement higher than we are at the state and at the federal level, and thinking about re-allocation of resources. We can't get there if we keep cutting budgets. It's just unrealistic to think that we can get where we need to be—the 60% goal—if we keep balancing state budget cuts on the backs of higher education. We can't "efficient" our way to the Big Goal.

On the other hand, we are trying to start a smart conversation about, "How are we spending the money we currently have in higher education? Are there ways to spend it that better target student success as a priority?" I think we are seeing some uptake on that conversation. In the past, if you brought up the issue of productivity (and it's still true in some sections with some folks), you were almost driven from the room as the hackles raised. But I think we're seeing now, in large part because of the dramatic fiscal challenges being presented by the current economic situation, more receptivity to thinking about how we redesign our business model and rethink how we deliver education, both on the academic and on the business side of higher education. How do we look at our data, better understand where we're spending our money, contain our cost drivers, think about ways to re-invest around our core missions? We're seeing more receptivity to doing that analysis. How do we do that in a way that increases student success and sustains quality? The promise of a more-educated population is an empty promise if we get there by providing them with some piece of paper that doesn't really mean that they've acquired the skills and abilities that they need to contribute. So productivity includes enhancing quality but it is also about increasing capacity.

Sometimes the issue of success in college unfortunately gets reduced to a graduation-rate discussion. Those of us who have been around for a while are all attuned to IPEDS and graduation rates.

I'm not saying that we shouldn't be doing better with first-time, full-time students and getting them degrees at higher rates and faster. We definitely believe that. What we're really talking about is expanding capacity and opening the doors of higher education to a much larger group of people.

My argument always is that if you only focus on graduation rates, and this is fairly obvious, I think—any president or provost in higher education that I've ever worked with knows how to increase the graduation rate of an institution dramatically. You only accept those students who are highly likely to graduate. That doesn't get us where we need to be. I saw some data on an institution the other day, where they have dramatically increased their graduation rate but the actual number of degrees they're producing has gone down, and that just doesn't get it.

We still see folks who believe that the only way we can get there is with much more money, but those in government and business have a different view. As I said, our position is that we need an informed conversation and a partnership because it will take some re-prioritization of public resources around higher education— meaning more resources for higher education—for us to ultimately get there, as well as increased productivity with the resources we have.

Simply saying, "We can do it and we'll do business as usual, from a higher ed perspective—just give us more money to do more of what we're already doing," is not acceptable. There's never going to be enough money to get it done that way. So we have to have this productivity conversation. Our position is, "Higher education needs more resources to accomplish the goals that the country has set for it, but it also needs to do a much better job of utilizing the resources that it already has to increase capacity and quality and get more students to degrees." You need both those things to make it happen.

My experience with that statement has been, when I'm talking to one group of people, they tend to highlight the first part, which is, "We need more money." Then I talk to another group of people, and they tend to only hear the second part, which is, "They need to do a better job with the money they have and make it happen with that." We're going to give them a 20% budget cut and then we want them to move the number of people with high-quality, postsecondary credentials in our state from 40% to 60%. Neither of those are realistic by themselves. You need both efforts.

Pat Callan

President, National Center for Public Policy and Higher Education

Bill Patrick: What are the most fundamental issues confronting American higher education today, and how do leaders in government, business and academia see those issues differently than the majority of the general public does?

Pat Callan: Well, you can separate the major problems into two kinds. There are issues that are kind of internal to higher education and the way that higher education does its business, but the major problems, I think, are problems that are the consequences of external forces—the major demographic and economic changes that are taking place in the United States and in the world. There's the need to educate a lot more people with college-level knowledge and skills, and educate them better than we did in the old, post-World War II world. Those are the major forces that are changing people's expectations of higher education, and society's needs for higher education. We need to change the way that higher education thinks of itself and, in many instances, the ways that we do some of the business of higher education.

BP: Do you think the general public sees these problems differently than business, government, and academic leaders see it?

PC: We actually do a lot of public opinion research here, and I think there are some parts of this that the public sees more clearly than the academic and political leaders. I think the public understands, for instance, the widespread need to have some college, which I would describe as education and training beyond high school. In a field like higher education, you don't usually see big swings in public opinion, even over an 8- or 10-year period. And yet I think the biggest and single-most important change we see in America is . . . I think in 2000, we had 31% of the people in the country saying you need college to be successful in the workforce. Now it's 55%. That wasn't a one-time jump. We've been polling over this whole decade, and that went up steadily, every time we asked people.

Why? Well, because people on the ground, they see this economy . . . we're in our second recession in this decade, and they see that when the economy comes back, a lot of the old jobs don't, and the people who end up being able to function and get jobs that pay well and allow them to live a middle-class life are mostly people who have been to college. Or at least they're people who have had some education and training—more than high school.

But I think in many cases the political leaders (not President Obama, who has set this quite ambitious goal) but I think many of the political leaders, and certainly the higher education leadership, have generally not been quite as perceptive about what these changes mean.

What they really mean . . . in the post-WWII era, when we did educate more people to higher levels than we had ever done before—and that anyone had ever done in the whole history of the human race, really—in that world, people who didn't get a college education could still, if they had a good work ethic, get a job in a factory making automobiles or steel and have a middle-class income and buy a house in the suburbs and send their kids to college. That's the part of America that has disappeared.

In a sense, however we make the decision, when we decide who gets a college opportunity, we're really deciding who has a chance to be in the middle class. That changes in a very fundamental way the relationship between higher education and American society. We never designed the system to play that role, but that's what, basically, the marketplace is telling us, and that's what the public understands, I think, better than the educational and political leadership. The business leadership tends to be closer to the public on that issue, and they tend to see more clearly that educational requirements are going up and they're concerned about the workforce that they hire and the educational backgrounds that they have.

BP: But you think political leaders and educational leaders are, by and large, not seeing it the way those on the ground see it?

PC: That's right, although that's a kind of a blanket indictment. College leaders tend to be worried about the future of one institution—theirs—so these global issues maybe don't seem quite as relevant to them. Political leaders, I think . . . the ones that see it most clearly are the people who are seriously involved in economic development. I mean, governors who go on these trips around the country or around the world to try and bring employers in . . . the talk turns quite quickly on those trips to the quality of the workforce as one of the things that employers care about. It used to be that conversation was only about, "How good are your public schools?" Now they're about college, too.

BP: Is the current combination of continuing education programs at traditional schools, community college programs, non-profit institutions that serve adult learners, and for-profit, online educational businesses like Phoenix and Kaplan the right mix for accomplishing the president's degree-completion goal for higher education, or is that just a mish-mash?

PC: Well, we have a very heterogeneous higher education system. Some would say we're decentralizing to public and private and for-profit and non-profit institutions. We have 50 states with higher education systems that they're responsible for. We have a huge diffusion of responsibility in authority, and a mix of institutions that, as you say, doesn't always mix well. It's been a characteristic of American higher education that it's been defined by the marketplace as well as by public policies that, say, create colleges, or provide financial aid for colleges or for college students or whatever. I don't know whether this is the ideal mix, but this is the system.

There are four issues I think we have to address if we're going to be successful in getting anywhere near where the president wants us to go. First of all, we have to have better preparation. We have to have more kids graduate from high school and be ready to do college-level work. Secondly, we've got to have capacity—we have to have enough institutions that reflect the variety of goals and objectives and interests and learning styles that people bring to higher education. This is part of the capacity problem. I think that we need all the capacity that we can get. There are so many people who come to college with so many different kinds of aspirations, and different goals, that I think having an array of institutions is necessary. In that respect, we have a system that is somewhat defined by the marketplace—that is, the choices students make have a lot of influence on what kind of colleges and universities we have. Now, to some extent, public policy influences those choices by deciding which institutions are publicly supported and which ones you can bring financial aid to. It is, nevertheless, a kind of market-oriented system.

While I can't say that we have the right mix—and presumably that's a dynamic thing which changes over time as both policy and the marketplace adjust—I do think that we need the capacity that all these places represent. They may not all be doing everything as well as they should, or as well as we would like, but this is definitely a time when we need a lot of different kinds of capacity. We need it online; we need it in the classroom; we need academic; we need applied; we need community colleges; we need four-year institutions, public and private; we need the capacity that the for-profits bring in, as well as the private non-profits. I generally don't regard the heterogeneity—the diversity, if you want—of institutional providers as a liability. I regard it as an asset. But that doesn't mean I think that the system is functioning in the optimum way, in terms of serving students and the country. I do think we need all these different forms of education, both because of the magnitude of the educational challenges we face and because of the heterogeneity of the population that we need to serve.

BP: Let me back you up just a little bit. You were talking essentially about traditional-aged students coming out of high school.

PC: Well, only on the preparation side. Preparation is just one thing—we've got to get students better prepared. Now the third thing is affordability. We've got to keep education in a price range that people can afford. The fourth thing is, throughout all of American higher education, we need a greater emphasis on completion. That's always been the Achilles heel of American higher education. Maybe we haven't done as well as we should on access, but we've always been weak on completion, and the international comparisons show this.

Those are the four things that I think we need—preparation, capacity, affordability, and completion. The preparation issue applies primarily to the young people, so we have to be concerned about that. For the adults, we're going to have to be prepared to do things for people who haven't been in a classroom for a long time. I keep telling people who worry about whether we're doing too much remediation that I don't know whether we are or not. We're bringing people in because of the volatility of the workforce, and because of the ages that we serve now that we didn't serve a hundred years ago. We still have to work on getting people to the point where they can really benefit from college-level education if they don't come prepared. As for the young people, I think we should be concerned about the preparation they get in the elementary and secondary system. Many come to college unprepared to be successful. The other three apply to the whole population.

BP: Sure. That's a good point. What's going to happen if we don't make the president's goal?

PC: These goals don't come out of speculation, although nobody can really forecast what labor markets will look like. Yet, there are two reasons why I think we'll have a lot to worry about if we don't make the goal. Our last big transition in American higher education—our big era of change—came in the 1950s, '60s, and early '70s, as the baby boomers came of age, and that was when we expanded American higher education enormously. They were the biggest generation we've ever had. Higher percentages of them went to college, and we wanted to encourage that. That's basically when we created mass higher education—community colleges and other broad access institutions. What that means is that our largest and best-educated group of Americans is the baby boomers. However, as we speak, they are moving toward retirement. So we're now in an international, highly competitive, global economy, and who is going to take the places of those people?

At the same time, we've seen international comparisons which suggest that the United States has dropped from first—in the proportion that have access to college—to a tie for something around tenth place. As I mentioned earlier, we've never been high on the college completion list. If we look at our 25–35-year old workforce, in the OECD international comparisons that don't even include China and India, we're one of only two countries in which our young population is not better educated than our older population. Another way of putting this is that our educational strength is in the people who are retiring and who are closest to retirement. The rest of the world has made their gains more recently. We made ours in the 1950s, '60s, and '70s. They've made theirs in the last decade and a half. Their educational strength is in their young population, who will be in the workforce for the next 40 years.

There's a real reason to believe, given the relationship between having education and skills that are correlated with going to college, that we'll suffer a penalty by not having a competitive workforce that will allow us to keep the best jobs here in America. Those jobs can be moved around the world anytime a lot of these big companies want to do it. So it seems to me the real problem is the American standard of living: it's not just about the desirability of more people getting to college.

Yes, it's about opportunity. We'd like the next generation of Americans to have the same chances to have good lives and to be prosperous that the last generations have had. But it's also about the ability of the states and the country to compete in this global economy in which human capital is such a critical factor.

Dennis Jones

President, National Center for Higher Education
Management Systems — NCHEMS

Dennis Jones: I'm making speeches all over the place, saying, look, content's a commodity now. You can get it anywhere, free. Best in the world, you can get online, free. What you can't get is the high-touch part of it — the mentoring part — the part that helps you succeed at using that online content. And what you can't get is the credentialing. You can go get content from MIT, but you can't get the degree from MIT, okay? So what you get is mentoring and credentialing, and you get it from an institution that's passed all the tests for accreditation. And you can get it at a price that, depending on your style, is 6,000 bucks for however much you can do — not 6,000 bucks for 30 credits, which is pretty cool.

Bill Patrick: Do you think that most people in America think of an Excelsior degree or an Empire State degree or a WGU degree in the same way that they think of Ivy League degrees or well-known liberal arts college degrees or Big Ten degrees?

DJ: Well, not yet, but I think we're getting close. I'll come back to Western Governors University, because I know it better. There are enough employers out there who are seeing the graduates of these programs to be able to judge. Yet, it's a question of, how long does it take for the perception to catch up with reality? Excelsior and the other schools you're writing about, they're all giving good degrees, and it's hard to argue that they aren't delivering.

BP: They certainly seem to be rigorous enough. So what do you think the biggest challenges are for working-age adults when they try to go back to school?

DJ: Well, I think two things: one is pre-enrollment counseling. What additional skills do you have to have? And do you have to sign up for two years to do that, or can we find a fast track solution to that? I'm hoping that the returning student gets some clarity of purpose around this important first step. The advisors and admissions people have a really important job. The second step is matching a provider to that need. Who can do that for you? I think that content is a commodity, and what we're really selling is case management. How one bundles the case management role becomes essential.

The people that we're talking about, they're in the unemployment office. Unemployment offices are great for truck drivers and blue-collar folks, but they're not good at helping folks whose jobs got outsourced. All of the evidence that we can find says that the older the student, the more oriented they are to certificates, for obvious reasons. They want to get something that has economic return and they want to get it quickly. That means that even an associate's degree is a long time coming—two years—and that's if you're doing nothing but. So how do you take folks from where they are, get them a step up the economic ladder, and then keep them employed. The idea of stackable certificates is something we need to consider: you get this, you get that, and then you can put this on top, and you get an associate's degree. It's an aggregation of marketable skills.

BP: You know, I talked to Arthur Levine, and he said some of the same things you're saying about competencies, except he said that he thinks in the future, people are going to go to places like McDonald's University, or IBM University, or Boeing University, and they're going to get a one-year certificate in this or that. He said they're going to be like credit cards: people are going to have all these certificates and they're going to show up and say, "Well, I can do these things." Does that sound crazy?

DJ: No, but that would take as big a paradigm shift for IBM and McDonald's as it would for higher education. IBM and McDonald's, all those folks, spend a lot of money in training—most of it for management, and most of it is corporate-specific. They aren't really in the business of selling training for export, nor do they want to be. As a matter of fact, they would say, "Yeah, we'll do the stuff that's corporate-specific, but general skills? We expect society to do that for us, or the individual." I talk to my corporate training friends, and there are a set of things that they think have to come from the higher education enterprise, not from them.

Now, having said that, I think that there is the reality that one's going to learn some skills going through corporate life. You accumulate skills. But you've got to somehow get those assessed and credentialed. I don't think that IBM is going to be in the assessment and credentialing business. That's where the institutions that we're talking about— Excelsior and WGU and the others—have it figured out.

BP: So all this talk about degree completion now—we've got Obama talking about it, and we've got the Lumina Foundation talking about it. They want to double the percentage, right?

DJ: It depends who you're talking to. We've done all the calculations for the Obama administration, and for Lumina, so it's all our fault. We started long ago making the case that the United States— at that time, 8th in the world—was slipping. We started picking up the OECD data about six or eight years ago and making the argument that, "Hey, maybe we're not as great as we thought we were."

We worked with Pat Callan and the National Center for Public Policy and Higher Education. Our collective findings started showing up in his publication, *Measuring Up*. He ran around the world and made speeches about the growing problem those findings represented. Lumina picked it up, and they started saying, "What does this really mean? How do we translate this into what we can understand? How big a problem do we really have?" Then, because Lumina was tight with Obama's transition team, that language found its way into the president's first big speech on education.

One could spend forever arguing about the nits of the degree-completion goal, but I think it's a great communication device: it gets people's attention. I think it makes the case that we aren't keeping up. The language is morphing from degrees into certificates, which I translate into something less than an associate's degree, but still offers employer-valued skills. This is where the paradigm-shift starts. Although we're not that bad off with baccalaureates, it's sub-baccalaureates where we are most vulnerable.

Tony Carnevale at Georgetown will argue that it's middle-skills jobs that are the drivers of our economy. They're the ones where we're most wanting. That means, again, focusing on certificates and focusing on a set of really bundled skills that you can take someplace and say, "I can do this."

BP: Well, do you think all those numbers that show that we're 13th in the world or 8th in the world or wherever we are in any given year, do you think they matter that much?

DJ: I think they're a measure of education capital. I think education capital probably reflects the ability to economically adapt, and therefore the ability to economically compete. We're in a different cycle this time, and I believe it's different for a couple of reasons. One, the economic environment of higher education has changed in ways from which we cannot go back—in terms of cost and in terms of the states' ability and willingness to pay for it. I think the whole finance model is a harsh picture, and it's in the midst of a change.

Because there's going to be continuing pressure on the demand side, I think that we are witnessing probably for the first time that there's been enough supply and demand pressure to force a change in the paradigm. In every prior economic slump, if you listen to the Brookings folks and others, they say, "When economic slumps are driven, like they were in the '70s and early '80s, by fuel prices, or in the early '90s by the dot.com bust, the economy went down in a hurry but it came back in a hurry as well. Looking at history, lots of history, when the downside is driven by the collapse of financial institutions, as this one was, and the 1929–30 one was, it goes down in a hurry but comes back very, very slowly.

Today, we have an extended recession on our hands. You talk to the people who really worry about state-level finance, revenues, expenditure patterns, etc., they say, "Higher education? We're not going to get back to 2007–08 until maybe the end of the next decade. It's going to be a very long time coming."

BP: So is the sky falling?

DJ: The sky is falling if we insist on business as usual. For those who are willing to experiment or adapt to alternative ways of doing business, it's nothing but opportunity. One of the problems in higher education is that we are so stuck in having to do business the way we do business—full-time tenured faculty, in classrooms, three hours a week per course, Monday/Wednesday/Friday, although we don't do Fridays anymore. For those who understand the imperative for change in the higher education business model, this set of circumstances is nothing but a help. It gives them the excuse to argue for change that they couldn't muster otherwise.

One of the problems in higher education has always been that when things get tough, the first reaction is usually: "Go find more money someplace else." The easy one is to jack up tuition. The second one is to hit the alums, and that only worked in a couple of hundred institutions. The state appropriation versus tuition trade-off has been the age-old solution to a drop in public support. But everyone's getting poorer, and take a look at the population we have to serve—they're fundamentally poorer to start with. As we involve more and more students, we're going to hit more and more poor students, particularly in the young population. Somewhere between 40% and 45% of incoming students are coming from families in the lower quartile of income—Hispanic families in particular. So a tuition offset isn't the answer.

BP: Do you think the president's initiative is going to work? Let's say we double our degrees—or whatever number you choose—by 2020. Do you think that's going to work?

DJ: How do you define success, and know whether it's working? There are two definitions of, "Can it work?" One is, "Can you hit that target?" Or is it so ambitious that people will say that it can't be done. Our calculation is that it will take about 4% increase, year over year, to get there. That's not an undoable number, and it's certainly not so big that we can't get there. The question of whether educational attainment can drive economic recovery is the bigger question.

The market still values education. There is absolutely no evidence that there is not an appetite for a more highly educated workforce and population. I don't know what the limits are, but we haven't come close to hitting them. If you listen to the corporate world, and if you listen to all of the higher education roundtable conversations, some of the things you'll hear is that we've got high unemployment and we've got jobs going begging. The thing that hasn't been accommodated is the recognition that the jobs that went away are not the jobs that are coming back. The replacement jobs are going to be much higher-skilled jobs. Even in the same job title, there's going to be a higher educational requirement. It's going to be much more computer-driven, and much less just hands-on, can-you-do-it work. People are going to have to get more skills.

All of the data say two things. The one we always point to is the more education you get, the higher your salary. The thing with the data that we don't show is, the more education you get, the more likely you are to have a job at all, which is pretty essential.

Martha Kanter

U.S. Undersecretary of Education

Bill Patrick: Please start anywhere on that list of questions that you want.

Martha Kanter: I'll start at the beginning. I think there are three fundamental issues. I've been talking about these around the country. The first is access to higher education, and that ties into the capacity of institutions to accept and educate the full range of Americans—what I call the top 100% of Americans. This runs the gamut from the tiny little school with several hundred students in a rural part of the country all the way to the flagships in the urban centers that have been well-known for more than a hundred and in some cases several hundred years.

The access issue is really one of, I think, national significance. We're growing from 300 million to 450 million Americans over the next 20 to 30 years, and we've got to figure out how many students we're going to educate in traditional institutions. How can we leverage the capacity that already exists, and use the new capacity generated by the knowledge-economy, to welcome more students at a distance? I think that's been one of the hallmarks of programs like Excelsior and Western Governors and other schools that have moved ahead to really look at online delivery systems. University of Maryland has had long-standing agreements with the Army, and so on. It's a very exciting time for higher education.

We're going to be generating new ways of communicating. When you get an e-mail stating that the Association of Public and Land-grant Universities and Carnegie-Mellon are going to be producing easily accessible online materials that are going to use the best of cognitive science analytics, you know things are changing. You look at students texting each other: I was looking at three students walking down the street, and they were arm-in-arm, texting each other. We have to be cognizant that Americans are going to communicate differently, and figure out how we can leverage the ways in which they're going to communicate so that we can get them more highly educated more quickly. We have way too many under-prepared students who don't think that higher education is even an opportunity for them. That's why the delivery systems, the outreach, the marketing, and everything else are so important. If you've got people in the next decade who come in under-prepared, institutions have to think, *How are we going to get more people prepared more quickly so that they can do the college-level work to prepare for jobs that will be available?*

Part of your question—and I'm still on the access side—has to do with how leaders in government, business, and academia see these issues differently than the majority of the American public does. I think government—if you look at what President Obama has done—has put a stake in the ground with Congress. We have said that Pell grants are going to be available for students and will be funded over the next decade. Yet you have to figure out how to creatively fund everything that we're going to want to do, especially in this economic downturn. The savings from the new funding model, which will be direct lending—where the Treasury will write checks to students who go to college for their Pell grants—has allowed us to save $40 billion that we're reinvesting in Pell grants so students will have them for the next decade.

I think you've got a commitment there. But if you look back to when Pell grants started, Pell covered two-thirds of a degree's cost. Now Pell is covering just one-third of that cost. We're going to have to figure out what to do beyond the American Opportunity Tax Credit, which will give families a tax deduction for their children to go to college. Or working adults who go to college will get a tax credit. You can get a Pell grant; you can get affordable loans. But it's going to be difficult. It's going to be difficult unless we really address the affordability side of the equation. For us, access includes enrollment and affordability and all the constraints that institutions have to deal with. Academia and government have to look at: "How are you going to get in the door, and how are you going to keep the middle class engaged in a college opportunity and not shut them out because of cost?" I think those are big questions.

Another issue is how are you going to deal with the wide diversity of students, who learn differently, and who come from different backgrounds, and who can drop out in a second? We've got a huge crisis on the access side where we've got what many in the literature call "the revolving student." The drop-out student. I read an article some years ago on "the stop-start student." They start, they stop, they start again, they stop again, they change institutions. We've got to do better. We've got to give students an educational plan so they stay in school. That's one of the challenges for faculty.

Faculty have to do more, too. Everybody has to do more. Managers have to do more, to keep students on track. Students come from all walks of life, and many don't have the skills today to be successful. You can shut them out and say, "We're not going to enroll under-prepared students. Go somewhere else." But if there's nowhere else to go, then you create an under-educated population, which is what we have today. Shame on us for that. We have to have better gateways, and that ties to the next thing that I would talk about, which is quality.

Quality has to do with bridges, and I'll talk about that very specifically. We've got 93 million adults who have had little or no college, 75 million of whom are at basic or below basic levels of education. You can look at the National Adult Educational Statistics for that, if you want a reference. Given that, we have a national system of adult education. We fund school districts; we fund community colleges to do something that we call adult education. What we haven't done is demand a bridge between adult education and college.

We have to prepare students to speak English — to speak, write, and read our language — in adult education. Many people are coming here to become citizens, so they have to learn a basic level of education. We've got to bridge those programs into college-level competencies. That's where we have to call upon the adult education faculty and the college faculty to figure out where those gaps are and to fill them. It's not enough now to bring students to a fifth- or a sixth-grade reading level. We've got to bring them up through high school.

You'll see a lot of academics worrying about these bridges. From the under-educated American to the more highly educated American, we have a huge gap. Some of it is quality; some of it's not articulated properly; some of it's the content of our teaching. For example, Karen Gross, president of Southern Vermont College, found that half of SVC's students were not completing anatomy and physiology, and she's got a great nursing curriculum. So Karen got the faculty together to deconstruct the anatomy and physiology class, and then to provide intensive instruction over the course of a year, and to modularize it. Well, she doubled the completion rate and helped to provide a way around this big barrier to a healthcare career. It's that kind of quality-improvement work that's important.

Another quality effort that I think is very interesting is the Tuning Project, which the Lumina Foundation supported. That brought faculty together from a number of states to look at the competencies required in, I think, seven disciplines—English, history, mathematics, economics, and so on—and faculty from different institutions deconstructed what it meant to have a four-year curriculum in their discipline. How, for instance, is a freshman course in US history different than one that you would take as a senior? And what are the competencies required?

So they did that within a number of states, and then they brought the different faculties together, and they found tremendous congruence. The competencies included critical thinking, analytical reasoning, and the kinds of skills that you want students to have when they graduate from college. We have to ask, "What does it mean to get a baccalaureate degree? What does it mean?" Here we need to look at competencies. I think it also ties in with your question on prior learning: What do students know? What are they able to do? How can we document what students already know so that they are learning what they need to learn to be successful in work and in life?

Then the third part of my response is completion. As I said, too many students aren't finishing. If you look at the entire pipeline, in addition to adult learners, you look at 30% of children not ready for kindergarten; 27% of students are not completing high school. We lose a high school student every 22 seconds. And when you go up the line and see what's happening in college, in six years we're losing half of the students. In community colleges, we're losing three-quarters of the students. So we have a tremendous churning effect that we have to address. How can we get students back? What are we doing?

Look at Texas. They went after every student in the state who completed 100 or more semester units. They talked to them, and they learned that the students were satisfied with the education they obtained, but life got in the way. They had to work, they had to change jobs; they had to take care of their families; they had babies; they had all kinds of things happening. Texas has now gotten back half of those students, just by giving them different ways to get back into college and by providing a clear plan for what they need to finish.

What about the students who can't get through the first semester? We lose so many there. But there are lots of models now where I think we're starting to develop some insights. For example, how is it that Towson State in Maryland and George Mason University in Virginia have no achievement gap in college graduation rates? How is it that black and Hispanic students do as well as white and Asian students in those two institutions?

You've got to look at it in a number of ways. The completion problem is very complicated. Why don't students complete? There are performance-based scholarships; there's new research out of MDRC (Manpower Demonstration Research Corporation) and from Columbia Teachers College which says that if you give the scholarship money out at the beginning, middle, and end of a year, you'll get a higher completion rate, because it serves as an incentive for the students. If you give it all at the beginning, and it's spent in the first semester, then what?

I just think that we have to look at this in a variety of ways. You have to look at access, quality, and completion as a synergistic set of fundamental issues that have to be addressed together. In terms of adult learners, we have a long way to go. But we've got to find new delivery systems. I think we've got examples at Excelsior and at WGU and at other institutions across the country of how to accelerate student learning. It is about competency, and it is about solid, detailed, credit-for-prior-learning opportunities. Some of it can be tested out. They give you credit so you don't have to repeat what you already know.

On question three, the president's goal: The president is actually for an increase by 50% in the proportion of students completing baccalaureate degrees, but the goal is to move from 40% of Americans with baccalaureate degrees to 60%. Right now, we're 12th in the world when compared to developed countries that are part of the Organization for Economic Cooperation and Development (OECD). Canada is in the mid-50% range—55% or so—and they're at the top, with Korea and Japan and some other countries right below. The president has asked us to become first in the world. That means we would need to increase by 50% the number of baccalaureates between now and 2020.

You'll see a lot of emphasis on this in our grant-making. We're asking Congress for completion funds. The president came out last summer with the American Graduation Initiative, but that was only partially funded. We're going back to see what more can be done to make completion the highest priority in the country. If we're successful, that will improve quality and result in increased completion and job placement. We need to get America back to work.

I think the implications of not doing that is that we're going to get further behind. When you close down an automotive assembly line plant in Warren, Michigan and you transfer to robotics, and when you have people who have been on the assembly line for ten or twenty years, those workers need to obtain the new skills that are going to be required in transformational industries. If that doesn't occur, we're going to fall further and further behind.

We haven't focused all of our energies on helping students complete what they start. I think that's a huge problem. I do know, from having been a community college professor and president for 16 years, that life gets in the way. I know returning adult students, as well as high school students entering college, don't think of college as a responsibility. And people also don't recognize that more than two-thirds of America's undergraduates are working while they attend college. That's huge: the costs of going to college; taking care of all of your responsibilities; owning and running a car; transportation; childcare. I heard about those problems over and over again.

When I was a community college president, we set up an emergency fund, where many students on federal aid could come in and say, "My car broke down. I absolutely can't afford to get it fixed. Public transportation is going to take me two hours to get to and from school, much less work." I have a letter from a student who was a high school dropout. She had entered the community college, and she was a really bright student. She was dropping off her mother at her job; she was dropping off her brothers and sisters at their schools; she was dropping her kids off at childcare; and then she was coming to school herself. After that, she had to go to her own job, and finally pick everybody up again at the end of the day. So there are tremendous pressures on people today just to be able to live a middle class life in this country. I think that we think of college as a first-time, full-time, no-other-responsibilities, you're-going-to-go-somewhere-and-just-have-a-great-four-years-somewhere kind of time—and that just isn't the case.

The majority of American students are working, and they're going to school, and they're trying to make ends meet. We want them to be more full-time at school. We know from the research that the more full-time, the higher the completion rate. How can we figure out how to help them do that? With the downturn in the economy, people are working two or three jobs. We've got 2,000 drop-out factories across the country, in the form of high schools. And again, it's systemic. We've got to build a culture of completion, a culture of education. Education is a right; it's a precious gift that you have; you've got to begin and work hard and finish.

I think every institution, whether it's public or private, for-profit or non-profit, has a role to play in this. The right mix? I don't know. I know that we've seen a 20% increase in the number of students who have applied for Pell grants in one year.

Again, it was heartbreaking when I went with the president's entourage to the General Motors plant in Warren, Michigan. We met with some of the people who were not continuing on the assembly line, which was being shut down. There were going to be jobs in robotics, but the literacy levels and the training required to be successful in this modern economy were just not there. The education gap was huge.

These were people who were 40 to 50 years old, and older. They would have to go back to school and start a new career. Some of them were going to be able to do that—they were going to transition into healthcare (17% of the GDP today) and some other professions—but the bulk were not. Shame on us for not educating the last generation in the way that we should have, in a way that lets people transfer their skills across economic opportunities, so you aren't stuck in an assembly line job for 25 years and then have nowhere to go in a downturn. I think we can do better. The world is changing, and we need to change with it.

BP: That's a sad story. What did the folks that you talked to up in Warren say? What were they going to do?

MK: Some were going back to school. They were getting trade adjustment assistance funds. The community college was right there, trying to bring them in. If they needed literacy, they were trying to do literacy immersion. But you know, if you're not up to speed and you've got, say, an eighth-grade reading level, and you've got to complete statistics or calculus in order to be competitive, or anatomy and physiology so that you can go into some of the health-care fields, you have a problem. Many were just trying to get into entry-level certificate programs while obtaining more literacy skills.

Our population is under-educated, and we've got a responsibility. That's our concern in the office of Vocational and Adult Education. We are looking at career pathways for adults who don't have the necessary skills. We need literacy immersion in this country. In other countries, it's an expectation that you're going to speak two languages and you're going to speak them well. It's an expectation that you're going to write well, and that you're going to be able to do the math and the basics. Yet, many of the people in this country don't have the basics that we need to count on for the future.

What we want to do is to teach students how to maximize their human potential. Maybe I feel that way because Abraham Maslow was my teacher when I was an undergraduate. But I think that you have to be self-directed and think critically and have a strong work ethic if you want to be successful in whatever career you choose. People shouldn't be limited. We don't want people in dead-end jobs. We've already done that to the last generation.

We need to think about these pathways differently in society: they're doors to other things that you're going to have to do. The research is showing that students are changing jobs five to ten times in their lifetimes. Certainly I never thought I'd wind up in a government job in Washington, DC. But it's going to be more that way for younger people. And I think we have to change and modernize how we think about these things.

I think the best way to convince adults to enroll in higher education is to talk to them in their language about why they would want to spend their time in postsecondary education or in a training program. Right now, we have a lot of adults who are out of work. We can offer them short-term training, internships, apprenticeships, and opportunities for entry-level union membership. But it all depends on their literacy levels. Of the 75 million adults in America who don't have college degrees, many of them are at basic or below-basic levels of literacy. There are actually 93 million Americans, according to NIFL (National Institute for Literacy), who have had little or nor college. So, for the 75 million working-age adults without degrees, many of them don't even have certificates.

The whole economic condition of workforce is mobile, and it's changing, and people are going to have to have more than one job in their lifetimes. As a matter of fact, I think the data say five to seven jobs in a lifetime. One way to attract older workers back into school is to show them adults who have switched careers and have succeeded. We need to show them adults who have come into the adult education program in a local high school or community college and signed up for literacy courses. We could show them immigrants coming in who wanted to get citizenship, learned the basics, and then continued on to get their education. I think we need to explain what the multiple-career pathways are for Americans, wherever they start, at whatever level of literacy, and I think we're beginning to do that.

The other thing we haven't done as a country, that we really need to do, is ramp up literacy education so that it's delivered anywhere, anytime, anyplace. It should be high-quality, and you shouldn't have to wait for a program. The programs should be everywhere. We should have 24-hour television with beginning, intermediate, and adult literacy levels. We should have Internet components. I mean, there are radio literacy programs. We should just have a national campaign on literacy to address this.

We've got to do a lot more to get adults not only back into the workforce, but into the workforce to begin with. We need to show them the economic value of doing that, as well as the social and human benefits of getting further education. It's going to be about continuing your education from wherever you are. People are just going to have to get more education.

Arthur Levine

President, Woodrow Wilson National Fellowship Foundation

Bill Patrick: The last time we spoke, you told me that we were headed for a revolution in education. Are we immersed in that revolution yet, and how do you think higher education has been changed by it?

Arthur Levine: We are immersed in that revolution, and it's moving by fits and starts. Whether it's opening up courses online by major universities, or it's globalization of universities, or it's demographic changes, or it's competing universities in the private sector, or knowledge organizations like publishers, television, etc. moving into higher education, or whether it's simply the demands of a new economy to focus on new fields and new kinds of classes, all of it's happening. It's not going to be like the Berlin Wall, in which it all falls in one day and you wonder how it happened. It's going to occur over time, and it's going to occur with two steps forward and a half-step backward.

BP: And how do you think higher education is being changed by that?

AL: I think that what's happening now is, in many respects, higher education is confused and uncertain about what to do. We're all latter-day Rip Van Winkles: everything around us is changed, and it's not quite clear how we ought to react. One reaction is anger, where we say, "We're just going to keep doing what we are doing." Another response is to grab onto one of the changes—grab onto globalization; grab onto technology; grab onto new demographics; grab onto whatever. We're seeing many, many different reactions. Historians will look back and say, "Ah, yes, this was the age in which higher education changed." But it will be in fits and starts, and it will be on different campuses and in different places and different

193

states. A large part of that is the decentralization of higher education in America. That's the way innovation always occurs. It's the way we went from the college to the university, the way we went from the agrarian curriculum to the industrial curriculum.

BP: So during the next decade, what do you think the major challenges for higher education in America are going to be?

AL: Some of them will be financial—for both students and institutions. Let's say that a piece of this is going to be the new competitors; a piece of it is going to be students who have changed and are going to vote with their feet and choose the kinds of models they want. I'm going to stop and say those three major forces will drive the changes. If I had to pick more, I'd say it will also be government decreasing support and demanding increased accountability.

BP: That's certainly happening already.

AL: We talked about demographics; we talked about government; we talked about new competitors; we talked about the convergence of knowledge producers, and the new technologies that make possible all kinds of developments in higher education that don't exist at the moment. Textbooks will disappear. We will find that it's possible to create virtual realities, and you have to ask, "How does a stand-up lecture about fourteenth century Paris compare with actually taking students there, virtually? Why do we need a physical plant if we can have students on different continents feel like they're all sitting with each other in the same room, and who can meet with each other after class and work on projects together?" All of that is up for grabs.

BP: Do you think that in the next few years we will have three-dimensional e-readers that all college students will have to buy when they enroll in a school?

AL: I'm sure. Your professor will be sitting in your living room with you.

BP: I'm not sure I want that.

AL: Well, you have to get dressed.

BP: Yeah, exactly. I'd rather have my pajamas on. The next question has two parts: the first is—do you believe traditional higher education institutions are doing an adequate job of educating their primary students—the 18- to 22-year-olds?

AL: The 18- to 22-year-olds who are attending full-time and living on campus now constitute under 20% of all college students. So are they receiving a strong education? Yeah, those students are probably receiving the best education we have. The real challenge is the other 80%. Older students. The new majority—older, part-time, over 25—say that what they want out of college is convenience (offer classes at the appropriate time, when I'm available); good service (the registrar actually ought to be there to help me rather than to play gotcha); financial aid ought to be more predictable than playing the lottery. What they're saying is, "I want quality instruction, and I want low cost." We've seen over the last several decades that there's an exodus of students who ordinarily would have gone into higher education moving to organizations like Phoenix. If that isn't a mark that colleges and universities are not serving their audiences in the fashion in which they need to, I don't know what is.

BP: That predicts the second half of my question, which is: Can these traditional schools meet the needs of adult learners, or would the traditional system need a major overhaul to do that job?

AL: It's going to need an overhaul, but what we're seeing right now is three kinds of institutions—brick, click, and brick and click. The real battle is going to be over brick and click. We're going to have a small number of brick institutions that enroll students who are of the type that we talked about first. But what we're going to see now are institutions that try to re-formulate themselves. The institutions that are going to be most hard-hit by the loss of adult students to post-traditional sectors are going to be community colleges, regional universities, and non-selective private institutions, particularly in the Northeast, Middle Atlantic states, and Midwest. What's going to happen is we're going to watch the reforms and the adoption of the techniques that places like Phoenix have used in those schools first, and community colleges are well on their way to doing that.

BP: So how much of America's success in the next decade will rely on a much greater portion of adults earning college degrees?

AL: A whole bunch. The half-life of knowledge is getting shorter and shorter and shorter. The result is that more and more people are going to need to update and expand their skills and knowledge, and colleges and universities are going to be asked for a new kind of instruction. Don't give me just-in-case education—a whole bunch of subjects I might or might not be able to use. Give me just-in-time education: I need to have the following skills by Thursday.

BP: I'm laughing, but you're absolutely right. Well, Excelsior's tagline is: "It's what you know, not where or how you learned it." Apart from its marketing potential, is that concept workable in today's economy?

AL: Definitely. The reality is: tell me whether it's going to be better to have a degree from Microsoft or from Northwest State Regional University. So there are going to be brand names out there that will offer certifications which will matter more than higher education. That's never been true before.

BP: But are they all created equal? I mean, we've got Phoenix and Kaplan and Strayer and the for-profit universities that are online, and then we've got the schools that I'm writing about—these quality, not-for-profits, public and private.

AL: No, they're not all equal. All of traditional higher education is not equal; all the companies in the private sector are not equal. And it will be interesting to see who gets into this business. Remember that knowledge producers are converging. We will see publishers offering degrees, museums offering degrees, libraries offering degrees. What's a degree or a certification from the New York Public Library worth? What's a certification from Pearson's worth, or Scholastic?

BP: If you were in charge of a major university, how would you change it to fit your idea of an educational model?

AL: In 1828, the faculty of Yale was told by the state of Connecticut to get their house in order. The state refused to continue funding them because they thought the classical curriculum was worthless, and Yale did what colleges do when they're in trouble. They formed a committee. One of the things the committee wrote was: "How much do we need to change? Do we need to change a lot, or do we need to change a little?" And the state said, "That's the wrong question. The right question is, 'What's the purpose of higher education?'" Every institution has to ask that question. And given their answer, they need to build the institution that's going to achieve it in the twenty-first century. The state in 1828 didn't want a research university—they wanted a vocational university.

Fact of the matter was, in that period of time, Union College, which had a program in engineering, modern language, and science, had a higher enrollment than Yale and Harvard combined. The nation was changing, and people wanted different things. Like now.

BP: So do you agree with President Obama's new higher education plan?

AL: Yeah, I do. This is probably the most exciting administration I've seen in a very long time in terms of its educational agenda.

BP: Do you think his agenda will work?

AL: That's a whole other question. I think it makes sense, but we won't know whether it works for a number of years.

BP: Last question: If one of our passports to staying competitive with other developed nations in the world is the kind of credentials that places like Excelsior, or even Kaplan and Phoenix, provide, are they the best means of achieving it?

AL: Think of all the providers we just talked about. The choices that students have in this country are not only domestic universities: they're places all over the world. And what I expect is going to happen, given the diversity of providers, and given the different approaches they take and the length of their programs, is that we're going to have to move away from degrees and move toward competencies. That will be far more useful to employers anyway. What does a student know, and what can that student do? We're going to create the equivalent of passports that will stay with you throughout your lifetime and that will record all the competencies that you achieve over time.

What happens is, information economies care about outcomes. Industrial economies care about process. We have a university system that was designed during the industrial era — it's time-based; it's how long you're exposed to instruction. That doesn't make any sense. What matters is what you've learned. We're seeing that change in schools, and we're going to see that change in colleges.

Mark Milliron

Deputy Director for Postsecondary Improvement,
The Bill & Melinda Gates Foundation

Mark Milliron: Question one, about the fundamental issues, I would argue that we're in an exciting and challenging time—what some people would consider a dangerous time. You're seeing all the doom and gloom predictions about American higher education. People are rightly concerned: we've moved from 1st in the world to 12th; we are on the precipice of having the first generation which is less educated than the one that preceded it. So people are right to be worried. The canary in the coal mine is there.

What I think is happening now is you're seeing what classically happens in America, which is the reorganization of our educational system around our economy and our society. I am increasingly frustrated by people who assume that American education doesn't change. If you look at the last two hundred years, there's just no evidence for that: we invented land-grant institutions to expand our agricultural revolution and to begin the industrial revolution; we invented junior colleges at the beginning of the twentieth century to give more access to higher education; we invented vocational-technical institutes to give people pathways into the industrial revolution; we invented community colleges in the late 1940s into the 1950s, out of the Truman Commission—first time that term was ever used—and that was the bringing together of those technology institutes and junior colleges to create comprehensive, community-based colleges. And then in the 1960s and '70s, we opened community colleges at the rate of one a week. That's not to mention—just to go back to the K-12 world—we invented universal high school in the twentieth century. So we've seen a lot of change, and American education, in general, has done good work to try to adjust to our economic realities and the societal realities.

I think, in the last 40 years, we have been responding, on the societal side, to a real push for social justice, and on the economic side, the real push for more people to expand the Industrial Age and to begin new economies. After World War II and with the beginning of the Civil Rights movement of the 1960s, we had this explosion of focus on access in higher education. We poured all kinds of effort into opening access into higher education—a combination of expanding our public land-grant institutions, our community colleges. You saw the creation of new models of education for adult learners with the University of Phoenix and Excelsior and others. I think a lot of that was in response to the idea that we should give anybody and everybody a pathway into higher education. That was made even more acute, I think, in the late '80s and early '90s, as we began to move pretty forcefully from industrial economy into the Information Age.

Now I think we're at a place where we realize that access is important—and it's vital—but it absolutely is not sufficient. I think we're realizing now that completion has to be a part of the equation. It's not good enough to get people to higher education—to postsecondary education. You've got to get them through. So certification, diplomas, and degrees matter, because they give people choices, and because they give people pathways to possibility. Unfortunately, in the United States, the people who start higher education—that population looks like America—it's pretty diverse. However, the people who complete kind of look like the people who have always completed.

We are reorganizing ourselves, I think, in all sectors, around this notion of being much more forceful about the importance of completion. The caveat within that is that completion has to mean something. It can't be just giving people degrees. It has to be high-quality stuff—so the focus on deeper learning and the focus on life skills and learning skills really matter. The idea of quality is all within there. I think what we're seeing right now as the fundamental issue of American education, and in particular American higher education, is the reorganization of this family of providers that we have—that is everything from community colleges to universities to private liberal arts colleges, all the way through to the for-profits, really embracing this notion of how do you take that family of providers and ensure that in a given state, for example, that you have strong access, strong quality, and strong completion. Without those, you really are going to have some challenges societally, and you're going to have some challenges economically.

I think all of this is in some ways a wake-up call. I think what's happening is the business world, and the government world in some ways, didn't have to pay attention to higher education that much in the old economic model, because we didn't need that many people educated at a high level. But now it's an economic imperative that people get through, and so business and government are suddenly paying attention. They're frustrated because they're not seeing the outcomes that we should be getting and, again, it's causing this reorientation and reorganization and redesign work within the education family. It's going to be a difficult time, because all these sectors think they have the right answer. So you're seeing this clash of ideas, of people trying to figure out the way for this to work. My greatest concern, in fact, is that I'm really terrified we're going to end up in a conversation about the one best way. The power of American higher education is the diversity of higher education institutions that we have. They serve different functions and different roles. If we lose that, we're going to have some real challenges.

Bill Patrick: In light of all that, do you think the traditional institutions are doing it? Do you think they're really educating these people who haven't completed their educations?

MM: Well, let's go back. One, I think traditional educational institutions, broadly defined, are waking up to the importance of completion, and they have some work to do to get completion right—in particular, completion for low-income young adults. If you come from a college-going family, you're likely to complete. But if you're a first-in-your-family-to-go-on-to-higher-education student, you're going to encounter some significant difficulties. The research shows that if you're a first-generation student from a low-income family, and you test into developmental education, your likelihood of completing is in the single digits. If we really believe in the American Dream, we've got to take this seriously.

At The Bill & Melinda Gates Foundation, our approach is not about fixing higher education. Our approach is this: How do we leverage postsecondary's credentials to help people have pathways out of poverty? Our research shows that for low-income young adults in this country, the best way out of poverty—the game-changer for them—is some kind of postsecondary credential. We care passionately about that idea. I think we've got some work to do to try to get credential completion done well within traditional institutions, and I think that what you're going to see after that is a way to do this more broadly. What I would make sure we emphasize is that this can't be done by just redesigning or re-engineering existing institutions. Additionally, I don't think that this can be done just by welcoming transformative, new, innovative players to the market. I really think this is a both/and situation.

One big goal we have at the Gates Foundation is to double the numbers of low-income young adults who receive a credential by the age of 26, or double the percentage of those students who receive credentials. That's similar to Lumina's goal and to President Obama's goal. They're all pretty tightly aligned, in terms of the directionality of those goals. But our read of the tea leaves is that the only way we're going to get there is by really working with existing institutions to redesign and re-engineer, as well as by also welcoming new players to the table. It's evolution and revolution at the same time.

BP: I appreciate that and, once again, it's a great answer. But it's one thing for the Gates Foundation to talk about cooperation, yet most people I have been talking to have been mentioning the word "competition." How do you get past that competitive drive?

MM: Unpack what you mean by competition. I think there's a natural competitive environment in higher education between elite universities. There's a natural competitive environment in the for-profit world, particularly for adult learners. And there is a service orientation in a lot of the land-grant institutions and community colleges, where they're serving a district. There's even some light competition that comes from for-profits against them. I think competition is a dynamic in the field. I don't necessarily think that's unhealthy. It's just one of those things that makes people wake up and pay attention.

BP: I agree with you. I'm just hearing a lot of competitive talk from the people that I've been talking to about Kaplan, Strayer, Phoenix, Cappella. There's a pretty healthy competitive edge directed against the for-profits.

MM: Here's the challenge: I think everybody has data that they have to defend, right? So the for-profits really have to defend the debt load that a number of students end up with, and in particular, low-income students. I think the traditional institutions have to defend their low-completion rates and their inability to get people who are eligible for financial aid to actually get financial aid. If you're in a public university these days, the FAFSA (Free Application for Federal Student Aid) is like the new poll tax: it's the mechanism that keeps low-income people out, because they can't complete the FAFSA. It's supposed to be the very thing that gives them the financial resources that are the pathway to possibility. The for-profits have really innovated with this and they have great FAFSA-completion rates, particularly for low-income folks. That's a good idea that I think the public institutions could probably steal and do a much better job with. I think the competition effect is probably healthy. Without it, you get lazy. In education, there is enough challenge to go around. Everybody should pay attention to where they are losing students and to what strategies help more students get through. Our opinion is that we think that's a healthy dynamic within the market.

We're not going to tip the scales against one or for the other, but we definitely see the challenges within each of the sectors.

BP: Given the steep cuts in support for higher education during this current recession in America, and the responses to those cuts by traditional institutions, what do you believe the short- and long-term effects on the cost of higher education will be?

MM: This is tough. Our challenge right now is increasingly in the states. Specifically, you've got a war of priorities between healthcare and education. That's really what it comes down to, and in particular with higher education. It's not going to ease anytime soon. If you look at the spending on Medicare/Medicaid vs. higher education spending, the lines are going in opposite directions. Our challenge is going to be figuring out how we balance that investment. What's encouraging is that a number of states are saying the right things, trying to create more strategic pathways to funding within higher education, including things like outcomes-based funding or momentum-based funding, which we're fans of. I think that's going to be a big deal. But I do think we're going to have to take very aggressive steps within our innovation work not to assume simply that more money is coming. I think a fundamental belief of our innovation and redesign work is that more money is not coming. And so any of the innovations that we're doing have got to be undertaken with the same or with less money to achieve the same or greater outcomes.

BP: Dr. Brenda Dann-Messier of the Department of Education said recently that the 75 million working-age adults who don't have college degrees and are not presently enrolled in college are crucial to achieving the president's vision. In your opinion, what is the best way to convince those adults to enroll? How do we reach the other 80%, the people who haven't finished? How do we get those adults to enroll in our institutions, no matter which ones they choose?

MM: A few things: one, I think you have to go after low-hanging fruit. There is a whole array of adults who have amassed a number of credit hours that we should connect with and we should find out the ways that they can complete their journeys, in particular those who have left within the last six years. There are a number of university students who have left after 65 or 75 hours. I was just speaking to the American Association of State Colleges and Universities, at their summer conference with provosts, and one of the things we talked about was: Why in the world wouldn't you reach out to those students who have completed 70 or 80 credit hours and then had to drop out? Most of the time, by the way, they had to drop out because life happened. Reach out to those students and give them an associate's degree. Even if you have to partner with a community college because you don't have that degree-granting authority, partner with that community college and give them an associate's degree. The granting of that degree, if they've earned it — if their credit accumulation matches the degree — gives them a momentum point. It gives them a credential that gives them economic viability, and it makes it more likely that they'll come back to that academic journey. So I think step one is to go after the low-hanging fruit. Places like University of Texas, El Paso, and El Paso Community College have really done some good work in this regard. They have been reaching out and trying to make sure they connect with students around the possibility of earning an associate's degree.

Second is emphasizing the importance of education, and showing the different pathways for different kinds of learners. I think what happens is that many of them think that there's only one way in and one way out. They don't see the family of education opportunities that are right for them. There are some people who are made for the University of Phoenix; there are some people who are made for Excelsior; some who are made for Thomas Edison State College. And there are others who are really much better suited to a community college or to a state university.

Third is the need to reach the workplace. We do a lot of work on learn-and-earn in our portfolio, which is synching the workplace with education. Increasingly, we're seeing a number of employers who are trying to create pathways and programs so that more of their employees can get credentialed—even while they're on the job. You've got Northrop Grumman that has apprenticeship programs with local institutions, so that as they're training their employees they're actually earning credentials.

BP: Is President Obama's goal of a 60% increase in degree completion by 2020 a realistic goal, and if it isn't, why isn't it?

MM: Again, our data show pretty clearly that reaching these goals is absolutely unrealistic if you only do one or the other. If you only do radical, revolutionary new models and just focus on for-profits or just focus on transformative new techniques or technologies, you can't get there: you don't have the scale. If you just work on tuning existing institutions, you can't get there. It really has to be both. There is a pathway, but it's going to mean an aggressive focus on both ways.

BP: What about the implications of not making it? I know it won't appear as one big, single catastrophe, but what do you think is going to continue to happen if we don't really increase degree completion?

MM: At large, the notion that the world is getting more educated and smarter can't be a bad thing. I don't think that we can run around and publicly declare that it's terrible that people are getting more educated around the globe. We think that's great. The core mission of The Bill & Melinda Gates Foundation is that everybody should have the chance to live a healthy and productive life, and we believe that all lives have equal value. So for us to be advocates that we here in America have to be better than everybody else—that's tough.

What we do think is that we have to be in the game, and it would be great if we were near the top of the list, or at the top of the list. We think that the goal matters. We think that it should activate us and get us moving. We should be leaders in the world, in education in particular, and we want to be leaders in the world of education. So with that said, I think the challenge for us is going to be keeping our eyes on the prize. If we don't meet it by a discreet timeline, that doesn't mean we give up. We are in a learn-to-earn world, and that is not going to change anytime soon. For our country's economic viability, social well-being, and probably not only our international competitiveness but also our international relations, it's going to be important that we take education seriously. I don't think the sky will fall if we don't reach the goal, but I think it's absolutely worthwhile for us to go after it.

Louis Soares

Director of the Postsecondary Education Program,
The Center for American Progress

Bill Patrick: Can you focus on economic opportunities and challenges?

Louis Soares: Sure. When you say economic challenges, do you mean because college is expensive, or do you mean how the economy may not be growing as fast as it could if we had more educated people? Which one do you mean?

BP: I actually mean both and a few other things as well. Can we focus on the implications for our economy? For instance, if we aren't able to double the number of people who earn college degrees, or if the 75 million people who are out there with a high school diploma and various levels of learning—a few college courses, maybe low literacy and maybe not—what happens if we don't educate those people? What happens if we continue on the path we're traveling? When we slip from first place to tenth place in just a few years—where does the slide take us and what are the economic implications?

LS: The key challenge is figuring out the role of postsecondary institutions like community colleges and four-year schools, keeping in mind that normally we don't even think of community colleges in the same way we think of well-known colleges and universities. Normally, the thing that captures the imagination of the American psyche is the bachelor's degree at someplace like Harvard, even though that represents a tiny percentage of the people who go to college in this country. When you think about that, it has an important implication for the skills and economic productivity issue. For someone who goes to Bridgewater State College, I'm sure they're getting a good education, but they're not getting the Harvard experience, with all of the access that later comes with having gone to that school, right?

So when we talk about where we're educating the bulk of people, and when we say postsecondary education, what we're really talking about is this mix of skills that the economy uses in a variety of ways. One of our challenges in the US is that we haven't found the right way to translate credentials to the skills that the economy needs, right?

There is the "fit" of a bachelor's degree in a certain discipline with the needs of the economy. It's easier in the hard sciences, but even there it's tough. When you're talking about the impact of post-secondary education on economic productivity, we know at broad levels that there are connections. There are studies of regional economies which show that folks with more bachelor's degrees tend to have higher income, higher productivity, and tend to adapt faster to recessions. We know those things. But we really don't know a lot about the skills of these people. This is one of the core issues. Higher education institutions hide behind this a lot. They're like, "Hey, we're doing our job. We're producing credentials."

There is research that needs to be done around this. One of the challenges is that it runs up against some of our national biases. The minute you start talking about the purpose of education . . . I run into it all the time with my work, especially with higher education institutions. A lot of folks who are college-educated don't like the notion that the only purpose of higher ed is to serve the economy. They don't want it for their kids, who are in high school and intending to go to four-year colleges. It may be the case for those who are vocationally oriented, but clearly there are also a lot of others in the US who are not just looking for their kids to be trained as workers. They expect that people will become better citizens and better human beings by going to college.

This is one of the issues that we need to wrestle with. If I were thinking about a book, you'd have to say that one of our challenges is meeting our economy's needs through postsecondary education, because it also goes directly to the issue of working adults. We have to wrestle with this issue of why the public views our postsecondary system as a way to improve productivity and increase our ability to innovate. At the same time, we have to reconcile that with this other notion that college should also be helping people become better human beings.

In the US, we've tended to adopt this "Hey, we'll take care of you" attitude, but after K through 12, we're done with the total public-responsibility thing. After that, you're out in the economy on your own. We'll help you out with some financial aid, but you should be figuring out which skills you need, and how you want to get your education. That responsibility is on you. And when you move past the age of 22 or 24, you get into a space where you hear, "Okay, now it's all your responsibility. We might give you some help, but now you've got to juggle these things. Now you're an adult; you're an independent individual." It's always been very hard to develop a political constituency around this diverse group. You don't have a concentrated group saying, "Hey, we need help to get through at least one year of postsecondary education."

The governor of Michigan has a program called No Worker Left Behind. Essentially, the state of Michigan is investing a lot of money in basically making an associate's degree free—if you're either unemployed or if you have a family income that's below 40 grand a year. While they're moving some people through the system, they're finding it difficult for all the reasons I write about.

Once you get to be even 30 years old, and if you've been working for the most part since high school, even if you have some college, your self-image is more of someone who has a lot of labor market attachment and not so much that of a student. So it's very difficult for you—even if somebody is giving you free money—to be a full-time student. There's not enough money to go around, because even if the state pays for your full education, there are still your living expenses and incidentals that you have to cover, especially if you're married.

But it's also the psychology of it. It's very difficult to see yourself as a full-time student anymore. It's not how you conceive of yourself. You might not want to be full-time—maybe you do want to work. It gets messy. How do you combine work and education; how do you get paid; and how do you earn enough to cover your expenses, but not earn so much that you're ineligible for financial aid? It's very sticky. I'm trying to point out some of the institutional and individual issues that are aspects of our building a more educated workforce that leads to more economic productivity.

BP: I think those are great points, and they do underscore the complexity of this issue. Not many people have talked about it in this way with me, and all kinds of questions arise from it. If you're right that after K-12 ends, that people—and by "people" I mean taxpayers and the people who use tax money, like legislators and policymakers—if those people say, "Okay, you're 18 now and we've given you a public education, and we've given you a pretty good ride so far. You may end up at a community college, and some tax dollars go to support those; you may end up at a public university, and some of our tax dollars go to support those, too." But you're probably right, at least psychologically, that most policymakers feel like they have given students their shot and that they're now pretty much on their own. "Take a loan; do whatever you have to do. You've got to educate yourself at this point." Okay, that's that side of it, but of course once again, there are still those implications of elitism, classism, and racism that we have to talk about, because I'm not sure the majority of people feel the same about all of those 18-year-olds.

The other part that you were talking about—and that was also insightful—was how people in the workforce see themselves. I have a question about that. Working adults . . . okay, they've got their high school diplomas, and maybe they've gone to a college for a semester or two. They have a few courses under their belts; if they're in the military, maybe they've been collecting various courses as they move from base to base. What do these folks see in their future?

Everyone is exhorting them to get their college degrees, so if they go and get those degrees now, do they really think they have a chance to make more money? We're telling them that they're going to make more money, but they're also reading every day about how we have almost a 10% national unemployment rate, and they know how hard it is for many people to get good jobs these days. Should they really be taking the time, and spending the money, to get a college degree that might lead them to the same place that they're going to be at in four or five years anyway?

LS: You know, that's an excellent point. I want to take it up one level. A lot of the issues that I was inferring, and that you quickly picked up on, around class, relate to another, larger issue, which is the fact that these issues are why we don't have either a national industrial policy or a national human capital policy. When I first came to CAP (The Center for American Progress) about four years ago, one of the first things I said was, "We need a national human capital policy." And everyone said, "Oh, you're crazy. The Republicans will go ballistic, and we'll never get anything done." Not because CAP wouldn't prefer that, given our point of view, but if you lead with something like that, my colleagues were saying, you will get crushed almost immediately.

The fact is, we've never really discussed this at the national level. We have all this data that shows that an educated workforce is better for productivity, and that it's better for innovation. But we've never really turned around and said, "Hmmm, maybe we should have an approach—if not a centrally controlled approach—to this issue. Let's take a look at, and really think about, what is in our national interest." If you were to add up all of the 50 state approaches, do we have something that amounts to a national education plan that looks like it's trying to actually meet and forward that need? We don't.

We've begun to correctly identify the problem by manifesting it as an economic issue. The president talks about it a lot, or did, leading up to the American Graduation Initiative last year. But when you look at the American Graduation Initiative itself, and you look at where the money goes, the money goes into institutions. We say we're going to foment change and we're going to do pay-for-performance. Yet, grants have been coming from the federal level for years for this work, and we've never really turned the corner. Now, I think we're actually getting there. We might be at a tipping point, perhaps driven by the current crisis. Among all the issues that families are facing, there's this sense that we don't just need to get more bachelor's degrees for young Johnnies and Sallys, but that we finally need to be serious about providing them with some meaningful set of skills.

We have not made significant progress in forming a national human capital strategy. We are correctly pointing out the problem and looking at fixes, which in some ways is uniquely American. We're not France or Germany, where we think of things nationally and centralized. Until now, we've been unconsciously competent in getting people educated. But now, maybe we need to be consciously competent, because the rest of the world is catching up. We need to adopt a more thoughtful, long-term view about getting our human capital to a certain point of development.

I was talking to a business group recently. They want to do a forum in DC on jobs—there's a surprise! Everyone wants to do one of those. CAP is going to do one of those. But part of what I said to them was that I have been doing this work for a long time, most recently in the Clinton era. During that time, businesses got really involved with the Department of Education in creating career pathways. However, those businesses got co-opted into the details of those programs and the institutions. Instead of saying, "You know, based on our best bet, we need every adult in America to have at least one year of college education, and the credential associated with that should have some labor market value. We don't care about anything else." But I don't think you can get there without companies supporting employee learning and offering flex-time and various other forms of support and encouragement.

President Obama has set some goals for postsecondary attainment. The most interesting statement that he has made was to encourage the charge—it wasn't really a goal—it was the charge to every American to commit to getting at least one year of postsecondary education. One of the things I start my presentations with is, "What if the Pell grant had been designed for the purpose of getting every American through at least one year of postsecondary education, as opposed to getting a lesser number to four?" Really, the cultural intent of Pell was targeted on this traditional student who was going to get a baccalaureate degree. But what if the intention of it had been to get more people to the one-year level? What would our system look like now? I think it would be remarkably different. Think about the resources flowing to institutions that are interested in educating those people. I would argue that our higher education system would look very different today. Community colleges would have grown more. It's this notion of having something. I think the Obama administration has brought the right perspective in saying we have to expand our mental map to include a continuation of credentials. That's what opens up the opportunity to have a public dialogue about how we invest in all those different kinds of learners.

Margaret Spellings

Secretary of Education for President George W. Bush

Margaret Spellings: All right, your first question: *What are the most fundamental issues confronting American higher education today, and how do leaders in government, business and academia see those issues differently than the majority of the general public does?* Well, I think what we have in common is . . . all of us believe that education is important, and ever more so, all the time . . . a commodity in this global knowledge economy that we're in. I think Americans intuitively understand that. We have a lot of differences, clearly. I think leaders in government, obviously, are seeking accountability, transparency, and the best use of resources often, as is the business community. Academia, on the other hand, has loved and enjoyed the approach of, "Send us your money and leave us alone." That formulation has served them well these many years. So I do think there are differences between the sectors, and some of them are very acute. All of these players are driving the current debate.

I will say, if I do, modestly, that I created the Spellings Commission now—whatever, five-plus years ago—to start us thinking about these things, when it was quite unfashionable and when nobody was talking about them. I can tell you that I've had a number of people say, "Wow, I wish we had listened then." There are many in the academy who see what the Obama administration has put out in the way of education initiatives and think that it's a big overreach, compared to what we had offered. But, you know, timing is everything, right?

Bill Patrick: I think you were way ahead of the curve on many issues.

MS: Second question: *Why do you think we have lost ground in higher education to other countries?* I used to say in my secretarial days, "We love to run around saying we're the finest in the world." And that is true. I think we have the finest higher ed system in the world. But the question is not that. The question is: Is it fine enough for the changing world we're entering into? We've always done a darn good job of educating elites. We sure have. But that is increasingly not the game. So I think we have certainly lost some ground. Our competitors may be seeing the changes required better than we are. We're a little bit resting on our laurels.

Well, here I am doing all the talking. On the third question: *President Obama has set a goal for America to have the highest proportion of college graduates in the world by the year 2020, and until the healthcare reform compromise, his American Graduation Initiative was poised to spend $12 billion in helping us reach that goal. If you had proposed the same goal, what strategies would you emphasize?* Obviously, I did propose a lot of those same goals with the Spellings Commission. I think we've done a pretty decent job, notwithstanding all the complaining about affordability. We've worked on that in a bipartisan way for many, many years. We continue to pump money into the system, only to be met with increased cost and a lack of transparency. For me, the most powerful change that could happen is on the accountability and access sides.

Access is also a shared, bipartisan issue—when we talk about the need to have better-prepared kids and adults entering the system. But we're a long, long way from doing that. We have very limited accountability in our high schools. We have a lot of rationing of rigor. Why are we surprised that our kids are not college-ready when we learn that we have darn few qualified teachers for high-level courses—AP courses and so forth? I often used to make this comment: if you're at Langley High School in Fairfax County, there are twenty-plus AP courses; however, if you're at a public high school in inner-city DC, there are fewer than five. Then we're surprised that kids coming out of inner-city schools are not college-ready.

I think there's a lot to be done on the access side. But the main thing that I want to talk about is the accountability piece. We need more transparency and information and raised expectations and more consumer empowerment. These are the things that will build better incentives into doing the work of higher education. Today, we don't have any incentives at all for higher education to be more efficient, more productive, or cheaper. Out of the goodness of their hearts, they could do it, I guess, but there's nothing in policy that has said, "We want to see more of that."

BP: Why do you think that policymakers didn't listen to the recommendations made by the Spellings Commission?

MS: Because the academy was vigorous in its opposition. They love the, "Send us the money and leave us alone" idea. Well, don't we all? I'd like that and so would you.

BP: Sure. Do you think they'll respond any better now?

MS: I think they're more motivated. Yes, a number of the things that we warned about have become truer now than they were five years ago. Also, I think some of the things that we suggested seem more reasonable than some of the things now being proposed.

Let me see: *Dr. Brenda Dann-Messier of the Department of Education said recently that the 75 million working-age adults who don't have college degrees and are not presently enrolled in college are crucial to achieving the president's vision. In your opinion, why should they go back to school to earn a degree?*

Here's the thing—often I think we talk past each other about college degrees. This gets into the whole not-everyone-needs-to-go-to-college conversation. When we hear college, we think, "Oh, that's a four-year baccalaureate degree." But what we're really talking about is more people needing more postsecondary education. This we know for sure. Some people need baccalaureate degrees; others need postsecondary training and credentialing and certification and technical training that is different than that.

Yes, we need more education and more college degrees. But not necessarily for all. One thing we have to do, however, is—and this is where I think the for-profit industry has been innovative—we have to meet the customers/students where they are. If you want to contrast the for-profit approach with that of a traditional school, go to the University of Texas at Austin, for instance, but you better be available between 10 in the morning and 2 in the afternoon, and there you have it.

BP: Absolutely. Well, that leads into question #5, which is: *Near the end of September, the College Board issued yet another report showing that despite rising tuition and student-loan debt levels, the long-term payoff from earning a college degree is growing: workers in 2008 with their baccalaureate degrees earned an average of $55,700, which was almost $22,000 more than workers who had only finished high school. Do you think those numbers apply in our extended recession, when so many unemployed college graduates are out there looking for jobs, or do you think the earning gap will continue to provide a significant incentive?* There are a whole lot of people who may need degrees, but they might also be looking around and saying, "Well, I can't get a job now, so maybe I'll go back to school for a couple of years. But will I be able to get a job when I finish those two years?"

MS: Exactly. That's a legitimate question if you're going to spend a bunch of money doing it. It always struck me—and certainly the Commission Report says it—that one of the most important, most expensive, most impactful decisions that a family is going to make is about going to college, and yet often you have more information about your cup of coffee than you do about this decision. Our kids "get a feeling" about a certain school, and the next thing you know you're hundreds of thousands of dollars in debt.

BP: Why do you think that is? Why do people have more information about their cup of coffee than they do about college?

MS: We haven't provided families with much information about college. What we have provided is more around inputs, mood, and optics than it is substantive information. I think our consumers are starting to demand more. They want to know, rightly, what kind of outcomes they can expect for their investment. There is increased skepticism, largely because of affordability, I think.

BP: Well, questions 6 and 7 are related: *Would you talk about the role of for-profit colleges like University of Phoenix and Kaplan University, the current Congressional investigation, and the gainful-employment proposal?* And, *How are non-profit, credit-transfer and distance-learning schools like Excelsior and Western Governors contributing to higher education?* Can you talk about those two?

MS: Absolutely. I think we need all the help we can get; we need all hands on deck—for-profit, non-profit, trade schools, technical schools, you name it, to meet this challenge. We're far behind, particularly in ways that meet the consumer where they are, which traditional education is not known for. I really think that what the Obama administration has proposed in the new gainful-employment regulations is an overreach. They don't have adequate facts to base all this on. I hope in this delay that they've given themselves, they find a way to make these more useful. Which is not to say that we shouldn't crack down on people who are duping consumers, but there are already a number of tools on the books that allow the Department to do what has been proposed. I think we shouldn't kill the goose or geese. We need those golden eggs for the students.

BP: Do you think the administration is going after them because they're now creditors? They're lending out all this education money and they want to protect their investments?

MS: I'll let others answer that. I don't know what the possible motivations of the Department are. I will tell you that no Secretary—Republican or Democrat—over many, many years that this gainful employment provision has been on the books, has seen it as it is now being interpreted or has tried to take this approach. I can't speak to their motivation, but I can speak to the fact that this is highly unusual and, frankly, sort of extra-jurisdictional with respect to the

Congress. The Congress re-authorized the Higher Education Act, like it or not, not long ago, and they had the opportunity to weigh in on things like this and they chose not to. Congress, as we all know, is the primary policymaker for this sector and for our country. Anyway, I do think it's unusual, to say the least.

BP: How do you feel about schools like Excelsior and Western Governors? I know you just spoke to the President's Forum, and I just actually read the speech that your assistant, Nanci Danaher, sent up to me.

MS: As you know, I've worked for George W. Bush for a very long time, and I did even before I joined his administration. When he was governor of Texas, he was one of the founding members of Western Governors. I applaud institutions like Excelsior and WGU for being on the cutting edge of education. They are developing new and better ways to meet customers where they are, and doing it with others. That is a little bit unusual.

BP: What haven't I asked you that you think is important about these issues, and about working-age learners?

MS: Well, I think in some ways the public is ahead of the policymakers on all of this, which I have said in some of my speeches. People understand that they need this consumer good—this service that we call higher education. However, the days of higher education not being able to answer their questions about affordability, time to completion, and value are over.

Bibliography

Altbach, Philip G., ed., Berdahl, Robert. O., ed., and Gumport, Patricia J., ed. *American Higher Education in the Twenty-First Century*: Social, Political, and Economic Challenges. Baltimore: The Johns Hopkins University Press, 2005.

Baum, Sandy, Ma, Jennifer, and Payea, Kathleen. "Education Pays 2010: The Benefits of Higher Education for Individuals and Society." College Board Advocacy and Policy Center, 2010.

Berg, Gary A. *Lessons from the Edge*: For-Profit and Nontraditional Higher Education in America. Westport: Praeger Publishers, 2005.

Bok, Derek. *Our Underachieving Colleges*: A Candid Look at How Much Students Learn and Why They Should Be Learning More. Princeton and Oxford: Princeton University Press, 2006.

Bok, Derek. *Universities in the Marketplace*. Princeton and Oxford: Princeton University Press, 2003.

Brewer, Dominic J., Gates, Susan M., and Goldman, Charles A. *In Pursuit of Prestige*: Strategy and Competition in US Higher Education. New Brunswick and London: Transaction Publishers, 2005.

Brockman, John, ed. *This Will Change Everything*: Ideas That Will Shape the Future. New York: HarperCollins, 2010.

Brockman, John, ed. *What Have You Changed Your Mind About?* Today's Leading Minds Rethink Everything. New York: HarperCollins, 2010.

Carnevale, Anthony P., Smith, Nicole, and Strohl, Jeff. "Help Wanted: Projections of Jobs and Education Requirements through 2018." Georgetown University, Center on Education and the Workforce, June 2010.

Commission Appointed by Secretary of Education Margaret Spellings. "A Test of Leadership: Charting the Future of U.S. Higher Education." US Department of Education, 2006.

Duderstadt, James A. *A University for the 21st Century*. Ann Arbor: The University of Michigan Press, 2000.

Folbee, Nancy. *Saving State U.*: Why We Must Fix Public Higher Education. New York and London: The New Press, 2010.

Friedman, Thomas L. *The World is Flat*: A Brief History of the Twenty-First Century. New York: Farrar, Strauss, and Giroux, 2006.

Gardner, Howard. *5 Minds for the Future*. Boston: Harvard Business Press, 2008.

Gould, Eric. *The University in a Corporate Culture*. New Haven and London: Yale University Press, 2003.

Hacker, Andrew and Dreifus, Claudia. *Higher Education?* How Colleges Are Wasting Our Money and Failing Our Kids—and What We Can Do About It. New York: Henry Holt & Company, 2010.

Hersh, Richard H. and Merrow, John. *Declining by Degrees*: Higher Education at Risk. New York: Palgrave Macmillan, 2006.

Kamenetz, Anya. *DIY U*: Edupunks, Edupreneurs, and the Coming Transformation of Higher Education. White River Junction: Chelsea Green Publishing, 2010.

Keller, George. *Higher Education and the New Society*. Baltimore: The Johns Hopkins University Press, 2008.

Klein-Collins, Rebecca, Sherman, Amy, and Soares, Louis. "Degree Completion Beyond Institutional Borders: Responding to the New Reality of Mobile and Nontraditional Learners." CAP: Center for American Progress and CAEL: Council for Adult & Experiential Learning, October 2010.

Klein-Collins, Rebecca. "Fueling the Race to Postsecondary Success: A 48-Institution Study of Prior Learning Assessment and Adult Student Outcomes." CAEL: Council for Adult & Experiential Learning, March 2010.

Kronman, Anthony T. *Education's End*: Why Our Colleges and Universities Have Given Up on the Meaning of Life. New Haven and London: Yale University Press, 2008.

Levy, Frank and Murnane, Richard J. *The New Division of Labor*: How Computers Are Creating the Next Job Market. Princeton and Oxford: Princeton University Press, 2004.

Lumina Foundation for Education. "A Stronger Nation through Higher Education: How and Why Americans Must Meet a 'Big Goal' for College Attainment." Indianapolis, February 2009.

McMahon, Walter W. *Higher Learning, Greater Good*: The Private & Social Benefits of Higher Education. Baltimore: The Johns Hopkins University Press, 2008.

Menand, Louis. *The Marketplace of Ideas*: Reform and Resistance in the American University. New York and London: W.W. Norton & Co., 2010.

Muscatine, Charles. *Fixing College Education*: A New Curriculum for the Twenty-First Century. Charlottesville and London: University of Virginia Press, 2009.

NCHEMS: National Center for Higher Education Management Systems. "Strategies for Tough Times: The Reality of Higher Expectations." Delta Project on Postsecondary Education Costs, Productivity, and Accountability. NCHEMS, November 2009.

New Commission on the Skills of the American Workforce. *Tough Choices or Tough Times*. San Francisco: Jossey-Bass, 2010.

Percy, Stephen L., ed., Zimpher, Nancy L., ed., and Brukardt, Mary Jane, ed. *Creating a New Kind of University*: Institutionalizing Community-University Engagement. Boston: Anker Publishing Company, 2006.

Pusser, Breneman, Gansneder, Kohl, Levin, Milam, and Turner. "Returning to Learning: Adults' Success in College is Key to America's Future." Lumina Foundation for Education, March 2007.

Rose, Mike. *Why School?* Reclaiming Education for All of Us. New York and London: The New Press, 2009.

Smith, Peter. *Harnessing America's Wasted Talent*: A New Ecology of Learning. San Francisco: Jossey-Bass, 2010.

Snyder, Thomas D., National Center for Education Statistics. "Mini-Digest of Education Statistics, 2009." US Department of Education, April 2010.

Soares, Louis. "Working Learners: Educating Our Entire Workforce for Success in the 21st Century." Center for American Progress, June 2009.

Sperling, John. *Rebel with a Cause*: The Entrepreneur Who Created the University of Phoenix and the For-Profit Revolution in Higher Education. New York: John Wiley & Sons, Inc., 2000.

Steinberg, Jacques. *The Gatekeepers*: Inside the Admissions Process of a Premier College. New York: Penguin, 2003.

Taylor, Mark C. *Crisis on Campus*: A Bold Plan for Reforming Our Colleges and Universities. New York: Alfred A. Knopf, 2010.

Trachtenberg, Stephen Joel, ed. and Kauvar, Gerrald B., ed. *Letters to the Next President*: Strengthening America's Foundation in Higher Education. Los Angeles: Korn/Ferry International, 2008.

Trilling, Bernie and Fadel, Charles. *21st Century Skills*: Learning for Life in Our Times. San Francisco: Jossey-Bass, 2009.

Wolff, Daniel. *How Lincoln Learned to Read*: Twelve Great Americans and the Educations That Made Them. New York: Bloomsbury USA, 2009.

Zemsky, Robert. *Making Reform Work*: The Case for Transforming American Higher Education. New Brunswick and London: Rutgers University Press, 2009.

Acknowledgments

The authors wish to thank Alan Davis, Ed Klonoski, Robert Mendenhall, and George Pruitt, the presidents of Empire State College, Charter Oak State College, Western Governors University, and Thomas Edison State College, respectively, for their generosity and candor in the interviews they provided for this book.

We also owe a debt of gratitude to the higher education leaders who granted us interviews: James Applegate of the Lumina Foundation; Pat Callan of the National Center for Public Policy and Higher Education; Jim Hall, former president of Empire State College; Dennis Jones, of the National Center for Higher Education Management Systems, as well as his colleague there, Patrick Kelly, for important higher education data; Martha Kanter, the current US Undersecretary of Education for President Barack Obama; Arthur Levine, former president of Teachers College at Columbia University and current president of the Woodrow Wilson National Fellowship Foundation; Mark Milliron of The Bill & Melinda Gates Foundation; Louis Soares of the Center for American Progress; and Margaret Spellings, Secretary of Education for President George W. Bush.

In addition, we want to thank the graduates of Excelsior College who shared their life stories with us—Elizabeth Bewley, Chris Kilgus, Shannon McMillan, Daniel and Marcie Tulip, and Marie Wrinn—as well as the Excelsior employees who provided essential leads, important ideas, and continuing support: Mary Coonradt,

Betsy DePersis, Annette Jeffes, Laurie Keenan, Joseph Porter, Paul Shiffman, and Bill Stewart.

Finally, thank you to those friends who read our first draft and offered editorial advice: Quintin Bullock, Connie Cramer, Ed Klonoski, Carmel Patrick, and Dennis Unger.

About the Authors

John Ebersole is president of Excelsior College in Albany, New York. His career in adult, online and continuing education spans more than 25 years. Starting as an adjunct instructor, he has held leadership positions at such institutions as John F. Kennedy University, the University of California, Berkeley, Colorado State University, and Boston University. He is a past president of the University Continuing Education Association and currently chairs the American Council on Education's Commission on Lifelong Learning.

Prior to assuming the presidency of Excelsior, he held the Michael Sandler Fellowship at the Kennedy School of Government at Harvard. While in this position, he studied factors related to the acceptance of innovation in higher education.

John Ebersole celebrated his 67th birthday by completing a doctorate in law and policy at Northeastern University. He also holds an EdS from The George Washington University in educational leadership.

William Patrick is a writer whose works have been published or produced in several genres: creative nonfiction, fiction, screenwriting, poetry, and drama. *Saving Troy*, his innovative chronicle of a year spent living and riding with professional firefighters and paramedics, was published in hardcover by Hudson Whitman in 2005. A paperback edition of *Saving Troy* appeared from the State University of New York Press in 2009.

From his experience with the firefighters, Mr. Patrick also wrote a screenplay, *Fire Ground*, as well as a radio play, *Rescue*, which was commissioned by the BBC for their Season of American Thirty Minute Plays and aired worldwide on BBC 3. An earlier teleplay, *Rachel's Dinner*, starring Olympia Dukakis and Peter Gerety, was aired nationally on ABC-TV.

His memoir in poetry, *We Didn't Come Here for This*, was published by BOA Editions in 1999. In a starred review, *Kirkus* called the book a "marvelous memoir-in-poetry and a wonderful hybrid, written in a voice that's compassionate, fresh and American, without ever proclaiming itself such." An earlier collection of Mr. Patrick's poetry, *These Upraised Hands*, also published by BOA Editions in 1995, is a book of narrative poems and dramatic monologues. His novel, *Roxa: Voices of the Culver Family*, won the 1990 Great Lakes Colleges Association New Writers Award for the best first work of fiction.

Index